Guardians of Data

This book helps to reduce the risk of data loss by monitoring and controlling the flow of sensitive data via network, email, or web. *Guardians of Data* also shows guidance about data protection that data is not corrupted, is accessible for authorized purposes only, and is in compliance with applicable legal or regulatory requirements.

Guardians of data means protecting data, networks, programs, and other information from unauthorized or unattended access, destruction, or change. In today's world, guardians of data are very important because there are so many security threats and cyber-attacks. For data protection, companies are developing cybersecurity software.

The primary goal of data protection is not just to safeguard sensitive information but to ensure it remains accessible and reliable, thus preserving trust and compliance in data-centric operations. While data protection laws set out what should be done to ensure everyone's data is used properly and fairly, data protection is a backup solution that provides reliable data protection and high accessibility for rapidly growing business data. Data protection offers comprehensive backup and restoration of functionality specifically tailored for enterprises and distributed environments.

Guardians of Data

A Comprehensive Guide to Digital Data Protection

Nik Zulkarnaen Khidzir and
Shekh Abdullah-Al-Musa Ahmed

CRC Press
Taylor & Francis Group
Boca Raton London New York

CRC Press is an imprint of the
Taylor & Francis Group, an **informa** business

Designed cover image: Getty Images

First edition published 2025
by CRC Press
2385 NW Executive Center Drive, Suite 320, Boca Raton FL 33431

and by CRC Press
4 Park Square, Milton Park, Abingdon, Oxon, OX14 4RN

CRC Press is an imprint of Taylor & Francis Group, LLC

© 2025 Nik Zulkarnaen Khidzir and Shekh Abdullah-Al-Musa Ahmed

ISBN: 978-1-032-99530-4 (hbk)
ISBN: 978-1-032-99529-8 (pbk)
ISBN: 978-1-003-60467-9 (ebk)

DOI: 10.1201/9781003604679

Typeset in Palatino
by Apex CoVantage, LLC

Both authors dedicate this book

to their parents

Contents

List of Figures

Synopsis

In this book, readers embark on a journey through the intricate world of safeguarding digital information. Authored by industry experts, this book serves as a comprehensive manual for individuals and organizations seeking to fortify their defenses against evolving cyber threats.

The introduction lays the groundwork by emphasizing the paramount importance of digital data protection in today's interconnected world. It provides a brief outline of the book's contents, setting the stage for an in-depth exploration of various facets of data security.

The book begins by elucidating the nature of digital data, delineating its diverse forms and highlighting the risks associated with its exposure. It delves into the legal and regulatory landscape governing data protection, shedding light on compliance requirements and the ramifications of non-compliance through compelling case studies.

Readers gain insight into the ever-evolving threat landscape, from common cyber threats to emerging perils such as AI-driven attacks and insider threats. Real-world examples of major data breaches underscore the importance of implementing robust data protection strategies.

A plethora of data protection strategies is presented, encompassing encryption techniques, access controls, and disaster recovery plans. Best practices for ensuring security, including employee training and privacy by design principles, are meticulously expounded upon.

The book addresses the critical aspect of third-party risk management, guiding readers on assessing vendors' security posture and enforcing contractual obligations for data protection. Emerging technologies like blockchain and AI are explored for their potential in enhancing data security.

Rich with case studies and practical examples, the book offers valuable insights gleaned from successful data protection implementations and lessons learned from past breaches. Interviews with industry experts provide firsthand perspectives on navigating the evolving cyber landscape.

Looking ahead, the book ventures into the future outlook of digital data protection, predicting trends and innovations in cybersecurity. It concludes with a recap of key concepts, emphasizing the imperative of continuous vigilance in safeguarding digital assets.

An extensive appendix provides additional resources, including a glossary of terms, recommended reading, and tools for bolstering data protection measures.

This book is an indispensable guide for anyone committed to championing the cause of digital data protection in an era fraught with cyber threats.

Introduction

Welcome to *Guardians of Data: A Comprehensive Guide to Digital Data Protection*. In today's digital age, where data is the cornerstone of innovation, commerce, and communication, safeguarding this invaluable asset has never been more critical. Authored by leading experts in the field of cybersecurity, this book is designed to serve as your definitive companion in navigating the complex and ever-evolving landscape of digital data protection.

As we embark on this journey together, it is imperative to recognize the profound significance of our role as guardians of data. Every bit and byte of digital information holds immense value, whether it pertains to personal identities, corporate secrets, or the intellectual property of nations. Yet, with this value comes vulnerability. In a world rife with cyber threats ranging from sophisticated malware to social engineering tactics, the protection of digital data is not merely a priority—it is an imperative.

This is not just another book on cybersecurity; it is a comprehensive compendium meticulously crafted to empower individuals and organizations with the knowledge, tools, and strategies necessary to defend against a multitude of cyber threats. Throughout these pages, we will embark on a multifaceted exploration, beginning with a deep dive into the very essence of digital data.

From understanding the diverse types and classifications of digital information to unraveling the intricate web of legal and regulatory frameworks governing data protection, each chapter of this guide is meticulously structured to provide a holistic understanding of the subject matter. We will delve into the intricacies of encryption techniques, access controls, and disaster recovery plans, equipping you with the arsenal needed to fortify your defenses against cyber adversaries. But our journey does not end there. This book transcends theoretical discourse, offering practical insights drawn from real-world examples, case studies, and interviews with industry luminaries. Whether you are a seasoned cybersecurity professional seeking to enhance your expertise or a novice grappling with the complexities of digital data protection, this book is tailored to meet your needs.

As we navigate through the chapters, we will confront emerging technologies, trends, and threats that shape the cybersecurity landscape. We will peer into the future, envisioning the innovations and challenges that lie ahead, while equipping you with the foresight and resilience needed to stay ahead of the curve. Ultimately, this book is more than just a guidebook—it is a call to action. It beckons us to embrace our responsibility as stewards of digital information, to uphold the principles of integrity, confidentiality, and avail-ability in an increasingly interconnected world. Together, let us embark on this journey to safeguard our digital future, ensuring that the data entrusted to our care remains secure, resilient, and untarnished by the specter of cyber threats. Welcome to *Guardians of Data*. Your comprehensive guide to digital data protection awaits.

Authors

Nik Zulkarnaen Khidzir, PhD, is a Certified MBOT Professional Technologist, an Associate Professor in the Faculty of Creative Technology and Heritage, and Deputy Director of the University Malaysia Kelantan (UMK) International. His research interests include advanced methods for educational technology, multimedia and visual communication interaction in Islamic perspectives, software engineering, cybersecurity risks, information security risk management, entrepreneurial leadership, business and education computing/e-commerce and creative computing-related projects. As a founder of Cre8tivation Lab UMK, Universiti Malaysia Kelantan, he leads several high-impact entrepreneurship innovation projects and consultancy focuses on creative innovation and digital technology. Before taking an academic position, he had more than 20 years of experience in ICT integration entrepreneurship projects for government agencies, private companies and higher education. His niche area of research work focuses on creative innovation and digital technology. He has received various recognitions and awards in research and innovation competitions at the national and international levels. He was granted 10 IP for various innovations and inventions from technology research to innovative entrepreneurship education models, and he has written more than 70 journal articles, case studies, conference proceedings and other writings in the areas of applied digital technology, creative computing, entrepreneurship education innovation and cybersecurity. He is a member of the MBA Advisory Board (UniKL), the DBA Advisory Board (MIU), Master Trainer of Computational Thinking (MDEC), Professional Software Tester (MSTB), TTAC Auditor and member of the Panel of Assessment for Professional Technologist (MBOT). He received a top 2018 Outstanding Entrepreneurship Mentor Award from the Ministry of Higher Education Malaysia. He is a member of the Technology Advisory Board for Bayarcash, a digital financial merchant payment gateway online solution owned by Web Impian Sdn Bhd.

Shekh Abdullah-Al-Musa Ahmed, PhD, earned a BSc (Hons) in computing at UCSI University, Malaysia; an ME in information system security at Bangladesh University of Professionals (BUP); and a PhD at the University Malaysia Kelantan (UMK). He has written 19 research articles in peer-reviewed journals, case studies, conference proceedings, and other writings in the areas of applied digital technology, creative computing, entrepreneurship education innovation and cybersecurity. His research interests include advanced methods for educational technology, multimedia and visual communication interaction in education perspectives, software engineering, cybersecurity risks, information security risk management, entrepreneurial leadership, business and education computing/e-commerce and creative computing. His niche area focuses on creative innovation and digital technology. He has received various recognitions and awards in research and innovation competitions at the national and international levels.

1

Foundation of Digital Security, Understanding and Safeguarding Data

1.1 Overview of Digital Data Protection

Data protection legislation provides safeguards that support the development of the digital economy, while protecting the rights and freedoms of individuals in relation to their personal data. Personal data uses that are detrimental to individuals are detrimental to the digital economy as a whole. The concept of data protection is that personal data shall be processed in a manner that ensures appropriate security of the personal data, including protection against unauthorized or unlawful processing and against accidental loss, destruction or damage, using appropriate technical or organizational measures. An example of data protection is that data privacy is ensuring that sensitive data, such as financial information or medical records, is only accessed by authorized personnel. This can be achieved through access control measures, such as usernames and passwords, or biometric authentication. Encrypting data is another example of data privacy. So that the data protection law to make new provision for the regulation of the processing of information relating to individuals, including the obtaining, holding, use or disclosure of such information, and for incidental and connected purposes. Though the methods of data protection are:

- Encryption.
- Backup and recovery.
- Access control.
- Network security.
- Physical security.

Data on the go or in motion is typically encrypted on the fly. Examples of this include email messages, banking sessions via a browser, sensitive web-based applications involving confidential data, file transfers or downloads and information passed through virtual private networks, or VPNs. Encryption

DOI: 10.1201/9781003604679-1

FIGURE 1.1
Digital data protection.

is a vital component of cybersecurity that relies on digital signals (Figure 1.1). When data is transmitted over networks, encryption algorithms convert it into a secure format using cryptographic keys. This ensures that even if intercepted, the information remains unintelligible without the correct decryption key. Encryption uses an algorithm and a key to transform an input such as plaintext into an encrypted output and ciphertext. A given algorithm will always transform the same plaintext into the same ciphertext if the same key is used. Encryption works by encoding "plaintext" into "ciphertext," typically through the use of cryptographic mathematical models known as algorithms. To decode the data back to plaintext requires the use of a decryption key, a string of numbers or a password also created by an algorithm. 4G allows users to access the internet anywhere they receive signal. Fortunately, data being sent via 4G is encrypted, making 4G safer than public Wi-Fi. Now since the signal stores the data in an SQLite database encrypted with SQLCipher, the key for the database is kept in the key store provided by the operating system rather than a VPN works by establishing encrypted connections between devices. VPNs often use the IPsec or SSL/TLS encryption protocols. All devices that connect to the VPN set up encryption keys, and these keys are used to encode and decode all information sent between them. Since digital signals can be easily stored on any magnetic media or optical media using semiconductor chips, digital signals can be transmitted over long distances. However, the advanced encryption standard is a symmetric encryption algorithm that is the most frequently used method of data encryption globally. Often referred to as the gold standard for data encryption, AES is used by many government bodies worldwide, including in the U.S. Digital data recovery, also referred to as digital forensics, is the process of recovering data from computer systems, storage media and other digital devices. The purpose of the backup is to create a copy of data that can be recovered in the event of a primary data failure. Primary data failures can be the result of hardware or software failure, data corruption or a human-caused event, such as a malicious attack like a virus or malware or accidental deletion of data. In this case, you press the Windows key, enter "Windows file recovery" in the search box and then select "Windows file recovery." A storage system can consist of disk systems and tape systems. The disk system can include HDDs, SSDs or flash drives. The tape system can consist of tape drives, tape autoloaders and tape libraries. SAN connectivity comprises hardware and software components that interconnect storage devices and servers. Consequently, data backup means creating a copy of the system data that can be used for recovery in case the original data is lost or corrupted. You can also use backup to recover copies of older files if you deleted them from system.

Forensic data recovery utilizes specialized techniques and tools to retrieve information from DBD, including hard disk drives (HDD), solid-state drives (SSD) and other media. These techniques can recover data presumed to have been deleted, overwritten or destroyed. Backup and recovery is the process of duplicating data and storing it in a secure place in case of loss or damage, and then restoring that data to the location of the original one or a safe alternative so it can be used again in operations. Enterprise data recovery is the process of restoring lost, corrupted, accidentally deleted or otherwise inaccessible data to its server, computer, mobile device or storage device or to a new device if the original device no longer works. Data recovery is the process of restoring data that has been lost, accidentally deleted, corrupted or made inaccessible. In enterprise IT, data recovery typically refers to the restoration of data to a desktop, laptop, server or external storage system from a backup. Examples of logical data recovery include retrieving a corrupted document. Physical data recovery includes repairing a hard drive to recover its data. Instant data recovery incudes quickly restoring access to a database after a crash. After all the of data recovery such as logical data recovery, which addresses issues like file corruption, formatting and accidental deletion. Physical data recovery involves repairing hardware issues like damaged drives or broken components. Furthermore, data access control is a technique used to regulate employees' access to files in an organization. It involves leveraging the principle of least privilege (POLP) in managing employees' access rights based on their roles in the organization and defining and limiting what data they have access to. Digital access systems use electronic authentication mechanisms such as passwords, biometric verification, smart cards and other similar methods to verify the identity of individuals and grant or restrict access to the system. Biometric credentials are often used in access control systems in high-security spaces. Technology including fingerprint readers, facial recognition and iris scanning are common examples of biometric access control. The two main components of data access control are authentication that verifies the user identity, which could be done through a multifactor authentication mechanism. Authorization determines not only the level of access that each user has to the data based on specified policies but also the actions the user can take. Common practices for protecting data in use include tracking and reporting data access to detect suspicious activity and potential threats. For example, monitoring login attempts to platforms with sensitive information. Strict access control and Endpoint security management with authentication measures in place. When digital access is the ability to fully participate in digital society. This includes access to tools and technologies, such as the Internet and computers, that allow for full participation. A direct digital control (DDC) system is a solution that enables a sensor-equipped computer to automatically control a condition or process. It is typically aligned with a building automation system (BAS) and allows for precise control over heating, ventilation and air conditioning (HVAC) units. Digital control has the advantage that complex control algorithms are implemented in software rather than specialized hardware, thus the controller design and its parameters can easily be altered. The controller receives the encrypted tag number from the reader, decodes the number then compares the ID number to the ID numbers that have been loaded into the system. If the numbers match and the user is authorized to access the door, the door will then unlock. Data access controls are the mechanisms that limit or grant data access such as authentication, authorization, encryption or auditing. Data access permissions are the attributes that determine the level of data access, such as read, write, update or delete. Now that digital data is all information that is shared using technological devices, data includes photos, videos, text-based files, electronic books and newspapers. Security rules restrict harmful software and unauthorized users, allowing only authorized users with system-compliant devices to access files. Network access control also protects sensitive data from external threats and breaches when it is combined with intrusion prevention systems, DLP software and VPNs. Digital data has a vast range of applications. It is used in everyday activities like sending emails, streaming music and videos and using social media. In businesses, data and digital information helps in managing operations, analyzing market trends and making informed decisions. Furthermore, digital data is the electronic representation of information in a format or language that machines can read and understand. In more technical terms, digital data is a binary format of information that's converted into a machine-readable digital format, hence organizations are legally obliged to protect customer and user data from being lost or stolen and ending up in the wrong hands. Data cybersecurity is also crucial to preventing the reputational risk that accompanies a data breach. However, data in use includes all data that is accessed, processed and regularly modified by applications, users or devices. It is the state where data is most vulnerable to security risks due to the numerous threat vectors present when it is accessed or shared. Visibility of critical areas includes lighting and video cameras to monitor essential areas. Control can be accessed from simple locks through to keypads and biometric access. Perimeter protection is the traditional guards and gates aspect of physical security, so that access control measures ensure that access to physical locations is strictly managed and monitored. This includes locks, biometric systems, key cards and security personnel. Surveillance is the use of cameras, motion detectors and alarm systems to monitor and record activities. Physical security controls are designed to prevent unauthorized personnel from gaining physical access to network components such as routers, cabling cupboards and so on. Controlled access such as locks, biometric authentication and other devices is essential in any organization.

Whereas the golden rules of data protection are that necessary, proportionate, relevant, accurate, timely and secure. Ensure that the information shared is necessary for the purpose of where it is being shared, that it is shared only with those people who need to have it, that it is accurate and up-to-date, that it is shared in a timely fashion and that it is shared securely. Therefore, most data protection strategies have three key focuses:

Data security—protecting data from malicious or accidental damage.

Data availability—quickly restoring data in the event of damage or loss.

Access control—ensuring that data is accessible to those who actually need it, and not to anyone else.

The concept of data protection is that the personal data shall be processed in a manner that ensures appropriate security of that data, including protection against unauthorized or unlawful processing and against accidental loss, destruction or damage, using appropriate technical or organizational measures. Furthermore, data protection solutions rely on technologies such as data loss prevention (DLP), storage with built-in data protection, firewalls, encryption and endpoint protection. Everyone responsible for using personal data has to follow strict rules called "data protection principles." They must make sure the information is used fairly, lawfully and transparently and is also used for specified, explicit purposes, used in a way that is adequate, relevant and limited to only what is necessary. The CCTV data protection Act Information that contains the DPA Code of Practice from the

Information Commissioner's Office. This explains what the law requires if you have a CCTV system. The LED applies to personal data that is processed by organizations that are deemed to be competent authorities for law enforcement purposes. The purposes for such data processing include the prevention, detection, investigation and prosecution (PDIP) of criminal offenses, or the execution of criminal penalties. Data control is a business activity that encompasses the collection, storage and management of vast amounts of information generated within a company on a daily basis. This practice is considered one of the most important pillars for business success, providing essential guidance for strategic decision making. Finally, data protection is important, because it prevents fraud and cybercrimes. Applying strong data protection measures and safeguards not only protects individuals' or customers' personal data, but also organizations' data, therefore avoiding considerable problems, which may damage the organization's reputation or confidential information.

1.2 Importance of Safeguarding Digital Data

Data privacy safeguards individuals' personal information, preventing it from falling into the wrong hands. This includes sensitive data like Social Security numbers, financial records, and medical histories. Another important thing is to make security of digital data. Security of digital data is a robust data security management and strategy process that enables an organization to protect its information against cyberattacks. It also helps them minimize the risk of human error and insider threats, which continue to be the cause of many data breaches. Then there is the importance of safeguarding personal information. There is nothing more critical than keeping one's personal information secure to prevent identity theft. This information is the gateway to the person's financial institutions, medical records, credit score and other important personal records. The information needs to be protected in order to prevent that data being misused by third parties for fraud, such as phishing scams and identity theft. Data protection is also crucial to help prevent cybercrimes by ensuring details (specifically banking) and contact information are protected. The most important safeguard used in data integrity is backing up data. Backing up data can prevent it from being permanently lost and should be done as frequently as possible.

There are some practical steps you can take to improve your data security, such as

- Back up data.
- Use strong passwords and multi-factor authentication.

- Be aware of surroundings.
- Be wary of suspicious emails.
- Install anti-virus and malware protection.
- Protect device when it's unattended.

Data backup helps to protect against data loss by creating a copy of the data that can be restored in case the original data is lost. With business continuity, in case of a disaster or a system failure, data backup ensures that business operations can continue without interruption. Some common backup security measures include encryption of backup data, access control and authentication procedures, regular testing and updating of backup systems, secure storage and transmission of backup data and disaster recovery planning. The most reliable data storage and backup methods include cloud storage services like Amazon S3, Google Cloud Storage, and Microsoft Azure, which offer scalability and redundancy. Additionally, using external hard drives or network-attached storage (NAS) devices for local backups provides quick access to data. Making backups of collected data is critically important in data management to protect against human errors, hardware failure, virus attacks, power failure and natural disasters. Backups can help save time and money if these failures occur. Some types of data and sensitive research may have restrictions on where you can safely put data and its copies. Full backup is the most basic and comprehensive backup method, where all data is sent to another location. Incremental backup backs up all files that have changed since the last backup occurred. Differential backup backs up only copies of all files that have changed since the last full backup. It's a corrective control in ISMS (Information Security Management Systems). Controls serve a security objective and modify either the likelihood of occurrence or the amount of damage done. A backup does not prevent the loss of data due to an attack or a technical failure. Furthermore, hard disk drives (HDD) are the most popular data storage devices for home and business users. Hard drives are portable and affordable storage devices. Various other methods for data backup include physical media like CDs and external hard drives, hardware appliances, software solutions and cloud-based services. The choice of backup method depends on factors such as the volume of data, the frequency of data changes, the required speed of recovery and the available budget.

Multi-factor authentication works by requesting multiple forms of ID from the user at the time of account registration. The system stores this ID and user information to verify the user for next login. The login is a multi-step process that verifies the other ID information along with the password. Each account should have a unique password. Implementing two-factor authentication like combining passwords with an additional layer of authentication, such as a one-time password (OTP) or biometric verification, significantly strengthens security. Using MFA protects accounts by requiring a second form of verification, like a code sent to phone, a cryptographic token or a fingerprint, along with the password. This extra step makes it much harder for hackers to access accounts, even if they know the password. Authentication is the process that companies use to confirm that only the right people, services and apps with the right permissions can access organizational resources. It's an important part of cybersecurity because a bad actor's number one priority is to gain unauthorized access to systems The most popular multi-factor authentication technique today is sending a one-time PIN (OTP) to the user's phone number. Also, the stronger the password, the more protected information is from hackers, malicious software or cyber threats. Strong passwords are of the utmost importance in protecting electronic accounts and devices from unauthorized access, keeping sensitive personal information safe. The more complex the password, the more protected your information will be from cyber threats and hackers. Some people worry that multi-factor authentication is going to be inconvenient, it's generally only used the first time you sign into an app or device, or the first time you sign in after changing the password. After that, you just need the primary factor, usually a password. Authenticator apps are convenient, secure and free, making them a better option for MFA. Some password managers have integrated authenticator apps that will generate and store 2FA codes for accounts. The extra 20 seconds that you spend to receive a code via SMS adds a level of protection that can't get from a password alone.

Never click any links or attachments in suspicious emails or Teams messages. If you received a suspicious message from an organization and worry that the message may not be legitimate, go to your web browser and open a new tab. Then go to the organization's website from a web search. Email security is the practice of protecting email accounts and communications from unauthorized access, loss or compromise. If the message is illegitimate, contact local law enforcement or your local Federal Bureau of Investigation (FBI) office. Report internet phishing to the Anti-Phishing Working Group. Report spam, attempts to fraudulently obtain money or valuables and other criminal activity using the internet to the FBI Internet Crime Complaint Center (IC3). If the message is suspicious, you should report it; reporting a phishing email will help you act quickly, protecting many more people from being affected. The National Cyber Security Center (NCSC) will analyze the suspect email and any websites it links to. To prevent future spam emails, don't share your email address online, especially on public forums and social media. Spammers often harvest email addresses from these sources. Avoid giving it out to untrusted sources, and don't use it to sign up for online services or newsletters unless it's absolutely necessary. Look for inconsistencies or unusual formatting that may indicate a fraudulent message.

If the link appears dubious or redirects to an unfamiliar website, it's likely a phishing attempt. The purpose of a scam email is often to get you to click a link that will take you to a website that might download a virus to your computer or steal passwords or other personal information. This is known as phishing. Even if safeguard send for Microsoft 365 is a powerful tool that helps secure emails, protects against data loss (DLP), prevents PII and GDPR mistakes and avoids disclosing sensitive information that known in some circles as a spill, especially when sending emails to external domains. Suspicious email detection is a kind of mailing system where suspicious users are identified by determining the keywords used by a person. The keywords, such as "bomb" or RDX, are found in the messages sent by the user.

Antivirus products work by detecting, quarantining or deleting malicious code to prevent malware from causing damage to your device. Modern antivirus products update themselves automatically to provide protection against the latest viruses and other types of malware. Installing an anti-malware app and keeping it up to date can help defend your PC against viruses and other malware or malicious software. Microsoft Defender is free anti-malware software included with Windows, and it's automatically kept updated through Windows updates. Antivirus software protects devices from viruses that can destroy data, slow down or crash the device or allow spammers to send emails through your account. Antivirus protection scans files and incoming email for viruses and then deletes anything malicious.

Data security uses tools and technologies that enhance the visibility of a company's data and how it is being used. These tools can protect data through processes like data masking, encryption and redaction of sensitive information. To set these up, go to Start, then Settings, then Update & Security, then Windows Security, then Virus & threat protection. Under Virus & threat protection settings, select Manage settings, and then under Exclusions, select Add or remove exclusions. Select Add an exclusion and then select from files, folders, file types or process.

You should also avoid opening suspicious emails or downloading attachments from unknown sources. Additionally, you can use a firewall to block unauthorized access to your network. A comparison of the effectiveness of the 10 most prevalent antivirus products showed that more than 90% of the systems were protected by third-party software, revealing that the effectiveness of these products in detecting malicious software ranged from 90% to 98%.

Data security is vital for safeguarding sensitive information, ensuring compliance, building trust and maintaining a competitive advantage. By implementing effective data security practices, organizations protect their assets, reduce breach risks and establish themselves as trustworthy entities. Data protection solutions rely on technologies such as data loss prevention (DLP), storage with built-in data protection, firewalls, encryption and endpoint protection. Antivirus software serves a vital role in the Defense-In-Depth approach to protecting data on a computer system, along with other features such as firewalls and anti-malware software. It does this by scanning files and programs as they arrive on the device and determining whether they are safe. Different kinds of antivirus software do this in different ways. Some compare files to known viruses. Anti-malware can help prevent malware attacks by scanning all incoming data to prevent malware from being installed and infecting a computer. Anti-malware programs can also detect advanced forms of malware and offer protection against ransomware attacks. If you need to download something, you should use an antivirus program to scan that download for malware before opening it. Antivirus software also allows you to scan your entire computer for malware.

It's a good idea to run regular computer scans to catch malware early and prevent it from spreading. A robust antivirus software package is the primary component of technological defenses that every personal and business computer system should have. Well-designed antivirus protection has several characteristics. It checks any newly downloaded program to ensure that it is malware-free. Malware protection is a cybersecurity essential as organizations across all verticals host more of their data online and remote access and mobile device or personal computer use become the norm. It will shield you from the latest social engineering attacks and ensure that defenses evolve to match the attackers. Furthermore, these malicious programs steal, encrypt and delete sensitive data; alter or hijack core computing functions; and monitor end users' computer activity. Once it's downloaded to your device, malware protection periodically scans your computer to identify, quarantine and eliminate any malware to keep your systems secure. Strong passwords and software updates ensure all users create unique passwords and regularly change passwords. Use a password manager to make it easier to remember secure passwords. Malware attacks are best prevented by downloading and installing an antivirus program, which will monitor device activity and actions and flag any suspicious files, links or programs before they become a problem. Backup processes and testing restoration procedures are critical to protect against data loss. A world of fast-moving, network-based ransomware worms and destructive cyber-attacks must enable a data protection solution. This guarantees that you are always protected from new malware, even if it's not registered in the database of known threats. Adware Antivirus Free doesn't create a conflict if you have another antivirus program on your computer. Protective measures are prescribed to meet the security requirements such as confidentiality, integrity and availability that are specified for a system. Safeguards may include security features, management constraints, personnel security and security of physical structures, areas and devices.

As far as is possible, data security safeguards digital data from unwanted access, corruption or theft. It imparts physical security to hardware and software devices and covers all aspects of information security. It also imparts administrative and access controls and logical security to software applications. One example of a data safeguard, which is the most common form of this safeguard in an electronic environment, is the use of passwords. However, this could also include requiring proof of identification using tokens, biometrics, challenge or response scenarios, one-time passwords, digital signatures and certification authorities.

Data security safeguards such as firewalls are the initial security layer in a system. Authentication and authorization are two processes used to ensure only appropriate users can access enterprise data. Some examples of data security safeguards are: data encryption, data masking, hardware-based security, data backup and resilience and data erasure. Hence, the safeguards of sensitive data means:

- How to protect sensitive data.
- Take control of sensitive data.
- Encrypt data.
- Use a password manager.
- Backup data.
- Ensure the security of physical records and devices.
- Use a VPN on public Wi-Fi.
- Always stay up to date.

While there are some types of safeguards to protect electronic data, such as technical safeguards, the covered entity must implement technical policies and procedures that allow only authorized persons to access electronic protected health information (e-PHI) and audit controls. Hence, there are six protection methods to data security: by implementing robust data protection techniques such as encryption, access controls, data backup and disaster recovery, DLP, IDPS and employee training, organizations can fortify their data against potential threats.

1.3 Understanding Digital Data

Digital data, in information theory and information systems, is information represented as a string of discrete symbols, each of which can take on one of only a finite number of values from some alphabet, such as letters or digits. An example is a text document, which consists of a string of alphanumeric characters. Hence, digital data is, put simply, information stored on a computer system as a series of zeroes and ones. This means it's a binary language. There are three types of digital data: structured, unstructured and semi-structured. Digital data is any information represented in binary base 2. In this system, each column, starting from the right, represents an increasing power of 2: 2 to the power of 0, 2 to the power of 1, and so on. It is the language used in most present-day computers. Using digital data has a number of advantages and benefits, including increased accuracy, improved efficiency in data storage and retrieval, easier sharing of information across multiple platforms and more accurate tracking. Data processing is the collection and manipulation of digital data to produce meaningful information.

Data processing is a form of information processing, which is the modification processing of information in any manner detectable by an observer. An example is a text document, which consists of a string of alphanumeric characters. The most common form of digital data in modern information systems is binary data, which is represented by a string of binary digits (bits), each of which can have one of two values, either 0 or 1. As data storage can occur on physical hard drives, disk drives, USB drives or virtually in the cloud, the important thing is that files are backed up and easily available should the systems ever crash beyond repair. The earliest forms of digital data storage were punch cards and tape. Punch cards were widely used until the 1960s, when magnetic tape became more popular. These were replaced by floppy disks, then hard disks which could store more data, in the 1990s.

Data vulnerability refers to the weaknesses or flaws in a data system that expose it to unauthorized access and potential harm from cyber threats. Various factors are responsible for these vulnerabilities, such as software bugs, improper system configuration, lack of adequate security features or human error. A vulnerability is a weakness in an IT system that can be exploited by an attacker to deliver a successful attack. Data vulnerability has three categories: first, the data itself; second, the systems where the data is stored; third, the networks where data moves back and forth. If any of these is weak, that means data is vulnerable to attacks. Even the internet is inherently vulnerable to schemes like the XZ backdoor. Like so much else that it relies on, this program is open-source, which means that its code is publicly available; rather like Wikipedia, changes to it can be suggested by anyone. Big-data systems contain complex and sensitive data, making them prime targets of cyberattacks. Criminals can exploit big data systems to gain unauthorized access to data, disrupt operations or even cause financial damage. Network vulnerabilities come in many forms, but the most common types are malware, short for malicious software, such as Trojans, viruses and worms installed on a user's machine or a host server; social engineering attacks fool users into giving up personal information such as a username or password. Though vulnerability is most often associated with poverty, it can also arise when people are isolated, insecure and defenseless in the face of risk, shock or stress. People differ in their risk level as a result of their social group, gender, ethnic or other individuality, age and other factor. A vulnerability is a flaw or weakness in an asset's design, implementation or operation and management that could be exploited by a threat. A threat is the potential for a threat agent to exploit a vulnerability. A risk is the potential for loss when the threat happens. Physical such as theft, tampering, snooping, sabotage, vandalism, local device access and assault can lead to a loss of data or information. Environmental issues such as natural events like tornadoes, power loss, fires and floods pose hazards to the infrastructure in which data assets are located. Vulnerability information refers to the disclosure of security information about a vulnerability in a computer system. It is publicly available and published by trusted sources, providing details and risk ratings to help users assess their individual risk and take necessary actions to protect their assets.

The three states of digital data are a way of categorizing structured and unstructured data. These three states are data at rest, data in motion and data in use. Data can change states quickly and frequently, or it may remain in a single state for the entire life cycle of a computer. It can be classified into two broad categories, such as bitmap and objects: for example, image, video or audio files and textual objects, like Microsoft Word documents, emails, or Microsoft Excel spreadsheets. The benefits of digital data collection are—Improve data accuracy and digital data collection also eliminated data entry errors and data loss. Additional data can also be automatically gathered, such as username, geo-location and time and date. In the context of technology, "digital" refers to electronic devices and systems that operate using binary code, which is made up of ones and zeros. Digital devices use this code to represent data, such as text, images and sound, which can be manipulated and transmitted electronically. Digital data is the electronic representation of information in a format or language that machines can read and understand. In more technical terms, digital data is a binary format of information that's converted into a machine-readable digital format. Digital data can originate in two ways: it may come from a source that is inherently digital, such as a computer or messages consisting of written text, or it can result from sampling an analog message, such as voice. No numeral like 2 exists in the system, so the number two is represented in binary as 10, pronounced "one zero." However, the Latin digitus means finger or toe, so it makes sense that by adding the suffix -al, which means "being like," we get the adjective digital: "fingerlike." The idea of the word referring to numerals began around 1938 and soon became vital in computers. A digital signal represents data as a sequence of discrete values. The digital output is processed further by the aid of a digital processor included in the same microdevice or by using an additional microprocessor chip. Only a few microelectronic impedance devices are based on fully digital signal processing of digitized analog signals.

Computer storage and memory is often measured in megabytes (MB_ and gigabytes (GB). A medium-sized novel contains about 1 MB of information. 1 MB is 1,024 kilobytes, or 1,048,576 (1024 × 1024) bytes, not one million bytes. Similarly, one 1 GB is 1,024 MB, or 1,073,741,824 (1024 × 1024 × 1024) bytes.

Digital signals can be sent over transmission lines using either serial or parallel communication. With serial communication, the sequence of bits used to describe a value is sent along a single transmission line. As a result, data allows organizations to measure the effectiveness of a given strategy. When strategies are put into place to overcome a challenge, collecting data will allow users to determine how well solution is performing, and whether the approach needs to be changed over the long term.

2

Navigating the Digital Terrain

Understanding Data, Risks, and Regulations

2.1 Definition of Digital Data

Digital data in simple words is the electronic representation of information in a format or language that machines can read and understand. In more technical terms, digital data is a binary format of information that's converted into a machine-readable digital format. An example of data digital is a text document, which consists of a string of alphanumeric characters. The most common form of digital data in modern information systems is binary data, which is represented by a string of binary digits (bits), each of which can have one of two values, either 0 or 1. However, digital data is most often categorized in GIS as spatial (georeferenced vector or raster information) or non-spatial (tabular or attribute data linked to georeferenced features). Hence, the difference between analog and digital is in how the information or data is measured: Analog technology uses data that is continuous, and the goal is to capture a likeness of reality. Digital technology uses sampling to encode the data and then reproduces it as closely as needed.

Cloud storage is a mode of computer data storage in which digital data is stored on servers in off-site locations. The servers are maintained by a third-party provider who is responsible for hosting, managing and securing data stored on its infrastructure. A data cloud is an integrated data management system that unifies all the data sources, data stores and supporting data infrastructure in an enterprise. Most large organizations have complex IT infrastructures that can consist of multiple cloud service providers, on-premises resources and legacy software. A cloud database is a database built to run in a public or hybrid cloud environment to help organize, store and manage data within an organization. Cloud databases can be offered as a managed database-as-a-service (DBaaS) or deployed on a cloud-based virtual machine (VM) and self-managed by an in-house IT team. When using a cloud provider to host data or applications, this will reside on physical storage and

DOI: 10.1201/9781003604679-2

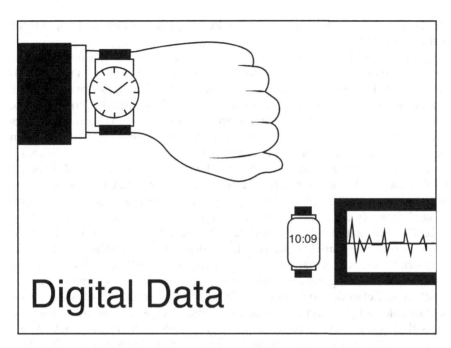

FIGURE 2.1
Understanding of digital data.

physical servers, and be moved around via physical networks, all housed inside one or more physical data centers (Figure 2.1). Microsoft Azure is an example of a public cloud.

With a public cloud, all hardware, software and other supporting infrastructure is owned and managed by the cloud provider, so these services can be accessed and the account managed using a web browser. A data cloud unifies structured, unstructured or semi-structured data to reduce complexity and simplify discovering data. Therefore, data clouds should be capable of collecting, ingesting and processing data from multiple on-premises or cloud-based source systems and serving it to one place. Furthermore, the cloud is called the cloud because it involves using a network of remote servers to store, manage and process data, instead of doing everything on a local server or personal computer. However, cloud services are application and infrastructure resources that exist on the Internet. Third-party providers contract with subscribers for these services, allowing customers to leverage powerful computing resources without having to purchase or maintain hardware and software. While cloud storage focuses on team collaboration, a digital distribution platform enables secure distribution of final content to the audience. The definition of the cloud can seem murky, but essentially, it's a term used to describe a global network of servers, each with a unique function. The cloud is not a physical entity, but is instead a vast network of remote servers around the globe which are hooked together and meant to operate as a single ecosystem.

In SaaS, the cloud provider is typically the owner of the data. This is because the user is using a software application that is hosted on the provider's servers. The provider is responsible for maintaining the software and the underlying infrastructure, and the user typically has limited control over the data. Blockchain technology is an advanced database mechanism that allows transparent information sharing within a business network. A blockchain database stores data in blocks that are linked together in a chain. Although blockchain is a type of shared database that differs from a typical database in the way it stores information, blockchains store data in blocks linked together via cryptography. Different types of information can be stored on a blockchain, but the most common use has been as a transaction ledger. A blockchain platform is a shared digital ledger that allows users to record transactions and share tamper-resistant information securely. A distributed network of computers maintains the register, and each transaction is verified by consensus among the network participants. There are four main types of blockchain networks such as public blockchains, private blockchains, consortium blockchains and hybrid blockchains. Block explorers are web-based tools that allow users to navigate through the blockchain's transaction history. For public blockchains, these explorers provide a user-friendly interface to access information like transaction details, wallet balances and block timestamps. Blockchain is a shared, immutable ledger that facilitates the process of recording transactions and tracking assets in a business network asset, which can be tangible, such as a house, car, cash or land, or intangible, such as intellectual property, patents, copyrights and branding. Bitcoin, launched in 2009 on the Bitcoin blockchain, was the first cryptocurrency and popular application to successfully use blockchain. As a result, blockchain has been most often associated with Bitcoin and alternatives such as Dogecoin and Bitcoin Cash, which both use public ledgers.

The tax definition of a digital asset is any digital representation of value recorded on a cryptographically secured, distributed ledger of blockchain or similar technology. Thus, blockchain will be increasingly improved in the field of technology and applied more deeply in a variety of fields and industries. AI data analytics refers to the practice of using artificial intelligence (AI) to analyze large data sets, simplify and scale trends and uncover insights for data analysts. AI is a set of technologies that enable computers to perform a variety of advanced functions, including the ability to see, understand and translate spoken and written language, analyze data, make recommendations and more. AI tools work by using algorithms to process large amounts of data, which help these tools learn how to do tasks similarly to humans. All AI tools first gain their knowledge from being trained on data specific to the tasks they're built for. AI can automate routine, repetitive and often tedious tasks including digital tasks such as data collection, entering and preprocessing and physical tasks such as warehouse stock-picking and manufacturing processes. Weak artificial intelligence, also called narrow AI, is a type of artificial intelligence that is limited to a specific or narrow area. Weak AI simulates human cognition. It has the potential to benefit society by automating time-consuming tasks and by analyzing data in ways that humans sometimes can't. AI models or artificial intelligence models are programs that detect specific patterns using a collection of data sets. It is an illustration of a system that can receive data inputs and draw conclusions or conduct actions depending on those conclusions. Synthetic data is created by generative AI models trained on real-world data samples. The algorithms first learn the patterns, correlations and statistical properties of the sample data. Once trained, the generator can create statistically identical synthetic data. Digital data is the electronic representation of information in a format or language that machines can read and understand. In more technical terms, digital data is a binary format of information that's converted into a machine-readable digital format. Big data refers to extremely large and diverse collections of structured, unstructured and semi-structured data that continues to grow exponentially over time. These datasets are so huge and complex in volume, velocity and variety that traditional data management systems cannot store, process and analyze them. Digital data is all information that is shared electronically using technological devices. Data includes photos, videos, text-based files, electronic books and newspapers. Digital technologies are electronic tools, devices, systems and resources which generate, store or process data. Digital tools include social media, mobile phones, online games and multimedia. The term "big data describes" the vast and intricate datasets created in the modern world, which include everything from financial transactions and sensor readings to social media interactions. Big data is important because analyzing it unlocks information and insights that are beyond human perception and the ability of traditional database analytics. The term refers to the incredible amount of structured and unstructured information that humans and machines generate, such as petabytes, every day. It's the social posts we mine for customer sentiment, sensor data showing the status of machinery, financial transactions that move money at hyperspeed. Furthermore, big data is a collection of data from many different sources and is often described by five characteristics: volume, value, variety, velocity and veracity.

Whereas the important of Digital data is the paramount significance in the digital era. It is the fuel that drives the digital economy and powers the technologies that we use every day. Data is used to improve decision-making, create new products and services, improve operational efficiency, personalize the customer experience and monetize data. The three states of data are data at rest, data in motion and data in use. So, the example of digital data to analog signal is that the 4–20 mA involves turning digital parameters into corresponding analog value current. The theory of digital data to analog signal conversion is generating an equivalent voltage that corresponds to the binary value. So, the reason digital is called digital is that traditionally, digital means the use of numbers and the term comes from "digit," or finger. Today, digital is synonymous with computer. This continually drives the software industry crazy protecting its copyrights; it is nevertheless a major advantage of digital processing. Unlike analog signals, digital signals are not continuous but are discrete in value and time. These signals are represented by binary numbers and consist of different voltage values. Digital data refers to information that is represented by a string of discrete symbols. Each symbol can take on one of only a finite number of values from an alphabet, such as letters or digits.

2.2 Risks Associated with Digital Data Exposure

The risks of data exposure are that sensitive data exposure that can be financially costly to businesses and damage their reputation and brand. The type of data at risk of exposure includes financial reports, bank account numbers, credit card numbers, usernames, passwords, customers' personal details and healthcare information.

The most common technology security risks to avoid:

- Phishing.
- Pretexting.
- Malware.
- Online pop-ups.
- Outsourced IT services.
- Wifi and remote work.
- Passwords.
- Old equipment.

Websites may contain malware such as ransomware which can sabotage systems and organizations. Or they might be designed to trick users into revealing sensitive information, such as passwords for transferring money. Phishing emails can hit an organization of any size and type. When a cybercriminal successfully steals an individual's personal information in a phishing attack, they can use that info to pretend to be them. This can cause all sorts of trouble, like hurting their credit score and damaging their reputation. Even phishing is dangerous because it preys on human error and bypasses even the most robust technical defenses. Phishers can be lone scammers or sophisticated criminal gangs. They can use phishing for many malicious ends, including identity theft, credit card fraud, monetary theft, extortion, account takeovers, espionage and more. The problem with phishing is that attackers constantly look for new and creative ways to fool users into believing their actions involve a legitimate website or email. Opening an email like this is relatively harmless as long as you don't interact with it. Most viruses are triggered by downloading an attachment or clicking a link. If you opened an email you suspect is a phishing attempt, then do not download any attachments. Spear-phishing is when these emails and text messages are highly targeted to the recipient With the sensitive information obtained from a successful phishing scam, these thieves can take out loans or obtain credit cards and even drivers' licenses in another person's name. They can do damage to your financial history and personal reputation that can take months to unravel.

Checkpoint Research recently released its 2023 Mid-Year Cyber Security Report, which provides data about phishing attacks and other major cyber threats. According to the report, phishing attacks were one of the most common methods for spreading malware.

You should train employees to spot the warning signs of pretexting. Courses should run continuously, include real-world simulations and last only 10–15 minutes. Enhance simulation exercises with login banners and regular emails to keep staff alert. Deploy multi-factor authentication to guard against the risk of password theft. Pretexting is confined to actions that make a future social engineering attack more successful. For instance, by dressing up as someone from a third-party vendor, an attacker can pretend to have an appointment with someone in your organization's building. Pretexting is a social engineering attack where a cybercriminal creates a fabricated story to bait their target into revealing sensitive personal or proprietary information, sending money or downloading malware. This puts the target at risk of identity theft, financial fraud and future attacks. Key elements such as assessment and mitigation involve the practice of security risk management (SRM) beginning with a thorough and well-thought-out risk assessment. You cannot begin to answer questions until you know what the questions are or solve problems until you know what the problems are Many forms of malware may cause a device to crash and allow cybercriminals to steal or destroy data. At the very least, they can create performance issues that hinder effective use of the device. A computer worm is similar to a virus, but it does not require user interaction to be triggered. Malware attacks can crack weak passwords, bore deep into systems, spread through networks and disrupt the daily operations of an organization or business. Other types of malware can lock up important files, spam with ads, slow down computers or redirect to malicious websites. Some forms of malware remove defenses to allow outsiders access to information on the machine; some send login credentials or personal info to others without your knowledge; and some disable the machine, device or network, which can require a full system reset and a loss of data. Examples of common malware include viruses, worms, Trojan viruses, spyware, adware and ransomware. Malware that can use stolen system resources to send spam emails, operate botnets and run cryptomining software, also known as cryptojacking. Certain types of malware, such as computer worms, can damage devices by corrupting the system files, deleting data or changing system settings. Since malware includes various types of cyber threats such as viruses, adware, spyware and ransomware. Most often, the goal of cyberattacks is to use the malware for financial gain. By using devious social engineering tactics such as phishing, cyber criminals can gain illicit access to a corporate network. Malware authors employ evasion and obfuscation techniques to evade detection by security tools and antivirus solutions. Techniques such as code encryption, polymorphism and packing make it difficult for traditional signature-based detection methods to identify malware. Some malware can hack email accounts and use them to send malicious spam to any contacts they find.

In many cases, clicking on a pop-up virus will trigger a malware download. This may be ransomware, spyware or ironically, a virus. This malicious software can be used to steal personal data and even hold it for ransom where they force a user to take action, which is fine if they convert, but only exaggerates intrusion if they don't. Bounce rate such as quite often the action users take is to leave the site. Sometimes lose other potential leads, even if pop-ups generate leads, be losing others by interrupting user sessions.

A popup is usually a small window or banner that appears in the foreground while browsing a website. The website's visitor can then interact with this window if the pop-up contains a signup or contact form, a button, or a link. Scientific evidence shows that long-term exposure to certain compounds under certain conditions even to low levels of POPs can lead to increased cancer risk, reproductive disorders, alteration of the immune system, neurobehavioral impairment, endocrine disruption, genotoxicity and increased birth defects. In IT, the most common and serious risks associated with outsourcing are those that affect operations and transactions, the confidentiality of information, business continuity and regulatory compliance. More formally, risks associated with outsourcing typically fall into four general categories: loss of control, loss of innovation, loss of organizational trust and higher than expected transaction costs. It's no secret that outsourcing work can be a riskier proposition than keeping it in-house. In addition to the potential for poor quality and delayed deliverables, there is also the risk of losing control of important processes and functions. Outsourcing has disadvantages. For instance, signing contracts with other companies may take time and extra effort from a firm's legal team. In addition, security threats can occur when another party has access to a company's confidential information and that party suffers a data breach. Working remotely is convenient, but remote employees may unintentionally put their company's data and networks at risk. Unsecured wi-fi connections, unattended computers and data breaches are just some of the potential negative impacts a company may experience. In the remote world, there's no guarantee workers are maintaining their equipment with the same rigor. They could be using technology that hasn't been updated in several cycles, leaving them open to attacks. This is especially challenging in body environments. Even one of the biggest threats to companies' remote workforces is the ongoing use of weak, insecure or recycled passwords and login credentials. Failure to use secure passwords negates cybersecurity software and tools like firewalls and virtual private networks (VPNs). Additionally, the use of remote information technology solutions has increased the risk of cyber attacks, particularly with the rise of phishing, data breaches and ransomware incidents. For example, it can start with something simple, like checking work-related emails or spending more time completing tasks after hours. Sometimes you may spend more time handling work, reducing time for your home and personal life. The situation can cause burnout and lower morale. Remote workers are typically the first to face security threats. They're often the source of network security incidents that can ripple quickly through the rest of the organization. Even if you don't have remote employees, mobile devices like smartphones and laptops pose security risks.

Cybersecurity risk is the probability of exposure or loss resulting from a cyber-attack or data breach. A better, more encompassing definition is the potential loss or harm related to technical infrastructure, use of technology or reputation of an organization. Remote workers are more vulnerable because they often use personal devices and unsecured networks, making it easier for cybercriminals to access sensitive information.

Additionally, the lack of direct IT oversight increases the likelihood of security breaches. Common network security threats include malicious software, malware, phishing schemes and Distributed Denial of Service (DDoS). Many network security issues create the additional risk of regulatory noncompliance.

Brute force attacks are when cybercriminals use leaked or known login credentials from one platform's user IDs, email addresses, passwords or pin numbers to gain unauthorized entry to other accounts. The more a password is reused, the more opportunities there are for data and money to be stolen. If a reused password gets leaked as part of a data breach, hackers then have the key for other online accounts. Now passwords can be shared, guessed or stolen, which means they aren't secure. Over 5 percent of young people admit that they share their log-in details with friends, and 59 percent of respondents admitted to reusing the same passwords across multiple sites. According to the Verizon 2022 Data Breach Investigations Report, over 90 percent of breaches involved compromised credentials. People tend to use the same password to protect many online accounts. Some users even use the same password to secure their personal and work accounts. If a hacker successfully compromises a frequently used password, they can gain broad access to all the resources the password protects. After all, some of the risks of using default passwords are that attackers can easily find and access internet-connected devices that use shared default passwords, such as routers, cameras, printers, etc. And attackers can use brute force or cracking tools to guess passwords, especially if they are weak or common. Hence, security issues with one-time passwords sometimes have malicious attackers who will use phishing, so when you enter a one-time password, you are actually just giving it to the hacker to enter. There are bots created solely for stealing these codes, and there are also SIM swaps where an attacker can intercept the code. Attackers can often work out the new password if they have the old one. And users, forced to change another password, will often choose a weaker one that they won't forget. The most common mistakes include using easily guessable passwords like 123456 or "password," using personal information like birthdays or names, using the same password across multiple accounts and not updating passwords regularly. These practices make passwords more vulnerable to being hacked. Password managers can be a security threat if they do not encrypt their data. Hackers know that compromising a password manager is like getting the keys to the castle. Because of this, a strong encryption must be in place to prevent access to your saved passwords. Common issues include the use of weak or easily guessable passwords and password reuse across multiple accounts, making it easier for malicious actors to gain unauthorized access. Additionally, the prevalence of phishing scams and brute-force attacks means that even the most careful users can become victims. Outdated facilities and equipment can pose serious risks to operations, safety and profitability. They can cause breakdowns, malfunctions, accidents and compliance issues that can disrupt productivity, damage reputations and increase costs. Work equipment can cause injury in five main ways such as entrapment, where parts of the body could be caught in parts of equipment. Impact, where the body could be crushed by moving parts or by items being processed. Contact, where the body could touch sharp edges, hot surfaces or abrasive surfaces.

Equipment failure is defined as any unexpected malfunction or stoppage of equipment. It can lead to production delays, quality issues and safety concerns. There are many different types of equipment failures, but they can all be grouped into three categories: design failures, process failures and human errors. Information and communication technology (ICT) risk means the current or prospective risk of losses due to the inappropriateness or failure of the hardware and software of technical infrastructures, which can compromise the availability, integrity, accessibility and security of such infrastructures and of data. There are various types of vulnerabilities such as hardware, software, procedural or human, and these can be exploited or used by intruders or attackers. For example, in order to understand this better, a vulnerability might be a service of a computer system operating in a certain logical port.

New equipment is often more efficient and can lead to increased productivity. In addition, modern equipment may require less maintenance, reducing overall maintenance and operating costs. Another benefit of replacing equipment is taking advantage of technological advancements. There is one problem you should know about older computers: they can be more vulnerable to security threats because they haven't been given updates in a long time. This not only puts information at risk, but it can also make your computer run more slowly. Threat actors may have already reverse-engineered the software and developed exploit code, making it easier for them to compromise the system. Running outdated software may cause compatibility issues with other software and hardware, leading to data loss or corruption. Identify how the machinery is likely to be used and misused. Identify hazards in connection with the use and operation of the machine. Assess the level of injury or harm that can result from exposure to each hazard assess what safety measures may be used and the protection that can provide. Whereas Safety equipment refers to protective gear and tools that workers use to protect themselves from harm and prevent accidents while on the job. These items may include gloves, helmets, safety glasses, earplugs, high-visibility jackets, and respirators among others.

The main risks of digitalization can be identified as: cybersecurity: data breaches, identity theft and cyber-attacks and technological dependencies that can create vulnerabilities. Then the risks of online data collection would be profiling and discrimination: Excessive data collection can lead to profiling practices, where detailed profiles of individuals are created based on their personal information. This can result in unfair discrimination, such as denial of employment, access to services or opportunities based on discriminatory criteria. The risks of data privacy would be theft or manipulation of sensitive or private information, such as financial or health records. Computer viruses can destroy data, damage hardware, cripple systems and disrupt a business's operations. The use of electronic devices, particularly when connected to the internet, can pose privacy and security risks. Cyberattacks, identity theft, data breaches and online scams are some of the potential threats associated with electronic device usage. Examples of advantages could include that the digital information is stable because it can be stored reliably in computer memory, transferred easily and copied and shared rapidly. Disadvantages could include issues of easy deletion, security and theft. Digital data is of paramount significance in the digital era. It is the fuel that drives the digital economy and powers the technologies that we use every day. Data is used to improve decision-making, create new products and services, improve operational efficiency, personalize the customer experience and monetize data.

The digital surveillance economy creates threats to individual consumers in the areas of compulsive buying, netting higher prices, discriminatory decision-making by suppliers, decision-making by suppliers based on erroneous data and decisions by suppliers whose rationale is unclear and essentially uncontestable. For instance, medical conditions could be shared without consent, or banking data could be made available to third parties. Emails can be hacked. Identities can be stolen. The risks are more far-reaching than most people realize because of what might happen to data next. The risk of digital security refers to the potential for unauthorized access, disruption or malicious activities targeting digital assets, systems or networks. It emphasizes threats like malware, phishing and cyberattacks that can compromise data and infrastructure. Data breaches are perhaps the most common type of data risk that businesses face today. A data breach occurs when an unauthorized individual gains access to sensitive information, such as personal data or financial information. In essence, a digital footprint can act as a virtual paper trail, leading directly back to the system. This can expose you to many privacy risks, including cyberstalking, harassment and even physical threats. Therefore, internet users must remain vigilant and take proactive measures to protect their online privacy. Wherever data risk is the potential for business loss due to poor data governance. The inability for an organization to ensure their data is high quality throughout the lifecycle of the data. Data mismanagement and weak processes for acquiring, validating, storing, protecting, and processing data for its users. Consequently, the risk to the rights and freedoms of natural persons, of varying likelihood and severity, may result from data processing which could lead to physical, material or non-material damage, particularly where the processing may give rise to discrimination, identity theft or fraud, financial loss or damage to the personal information.

An important step in improving online safety in the education sector is identifying what the potential risks might be. In general, the four areas are content, contact, conduct and commerce, sometimes referred to as contract. Digital risk refers to all unexpected consequences that result from digital transformation and disrupt the achievement of business objectives. When a business scales, its attack surface expands, increasing its exposure to cyber threats. These include cybersecurity risks, the risk of non-compliance with data protection regulations and the risk of legacy systems.

While banks develop thorough plans for dealing with financial risks, they may not be aware of technological risks. Banks might face several challenges when they try to mitigate technology risks. Security risks fall into three categories. The three risk management categories are human threats, physical threats, and cyber threats. Now let's consider them from the standpoint of access control. Human threats, such as employees, may give authorization to the wrong person by mistake or on purpose. When some of the biggest data risks include unauthorized access and insider threats, weak or compromised authentication mechanisms can allow unauthorized users from inside or outside an organization to gain access to sensitive data and intellectual property. Digital operational risk refers to the possible negative consequences associated with a company's technology. Digital systems can fail due to misconfiguration, natural disasters impacting servers, or cyberattacks. Technical problems can lead to service outages and supply chain disruptions. Inattention to open government and democratic principles in the implementation of digital ID systems increases the risks posed by these systems data breaches and threats to privacy rights, exclusion of marginalized communities and co-optation to advance state surveillance efforts. Big data poses various concerns, notably privacy and data exploitation. Big data privacy concerns refer to the threats and risks associated with collecting, storing, analyzing and using vast amounts of personal information in the era of data-driven decision-making. Compromised digital footprints can lead to identity theft, issues with background checks and reputational harm. Ensure appropriate preventative measures are in place to protect the confidentiality and integrity. Integrity helps determine that information is what it claims to be. Social engineering attacks are a primary vector used by attackers to access sensitive data. They involve manipulating or tricking individuals into providing private information or access to privileged accounts. Phishing is a common form of social engineering.

2.3 Legal and Regulatory Framework

The legal and regulatory framework matrix category covers broad issues related to the laws, regulations and policies passed by governments, including stakeholder participation and input into the decision-making process; the impact, or lack thereof, of these government efforts on citizens; and mechanisms for citizens. The regulatory reporting framework aims to enhance transparency and ensure that co-origination transactions are conducted fairly and in compliance with regulations. Therefore, NBFCs must establish robust reporting systems to meet these regulatory requirements. The General Data Protection Regulation (GDPR) is a legal framework that sets guidelines for the collection and processing of personal information from individuals who live and work outside of the European Union (EU). Approved in 2016, the GDPR went into full effect two years later.

Regulatory data means any and all research data, pharmacology data, chemistry, manufacturing and control data, preclinical data, clinical data and all other documentation submitted, or required to be submitted, to Regulatory Authorities in association with regulatory filings for the Product (including any applicable). As a result, regulatory frameworks are essential to stimulate growth and competence of new technologies. Such frameworks are key when developing competence to handle research, innovation and commercialization in biotech. The regulatory systems for the biotechnology sector vary between regions and countries. Consequently, to design an effective regulatory framework, it is important to define a clear overall purpose based on a good understanding of the issues that regulation is intended to address and ensure a shared understanding of its purpose and intended outcomes. For example, the risk regulatory framework is an outcomes-based approach to assess both the efficiency and effectiveness of regulatory actions and outcomes respectively and to continuously improve. This framework forms part of our broader Risk Management. Furthermore, the regulatory reporting testing function is responsible for assessing the data quality and integrity of regulatory filings and detecting issues. Regulatory compliance reports demonstrate an organization's adherence to regulatory requirements. These

Guidelines for the collection
and processing of personal
data of individuals within
the European Union

FIGURE 2.2
General data protection regulation.

are for external compliance reporting and are reviewed by regulatory bodies for determining compliance status (Figure 2.2). These can vary per industries, applicable regulations and geographical locations. The financial reporting framework is a set of standards used to decide on the measurement, recognition, presentation and disclosure of all significant elements included in the financial statements. Financial reporting frameworks offer guidelines for creating financial reports. In addition, the main difference between financial reporting and regulatory reporting is the audience: whereas financial reporting is mainly targeted towards investors and creditors, the main addressees of regulatory reporting are banking supervisors. If a company handles personal data, it's important to understand and comply with the seven principles of the GDPR: Lawfulness, Fairness, and Transparency; Purpose Limitation; Data Minimization; Accuracy; Storage Limitations; Integrity and Confidentiality; and Accountability.

Incidentally, regulatory data protection (RDP) protects innovative companies' investment in generating this extensive body of data through a limited period of exclusivity on the data, starting from marketing authorization. As a result, the General Data Protection Regulation is the toughest privacy and security law in the world. Though it was drafted and passed by the European Union (EU), it imposes obligations onto organizations anywhere, so long as they target or collect data related to people in the EU. Furthermore, the difference between a conceptual framework and regulatory framework is that while the conceptual framework focuses on enhancing the quality and consistency of financial information, the regulatory framework ensures compliance with legal and regulatory requirements. Both frameworks play crucial

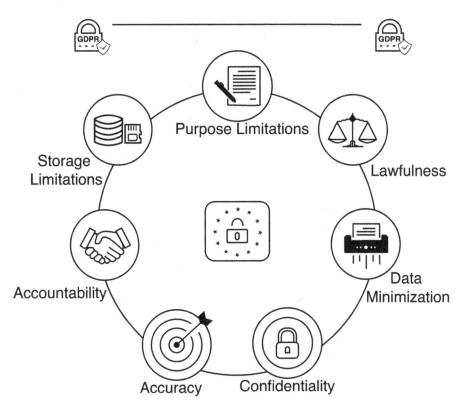

FIGURE 2.3
Seven GDPR data protection principles.

roles in the accounting and financial reporting process. Hence a "regulation" is any rule, regulation, order or standard of general application or the amendment, supplement or revision of any rule, regulation, order or standard adopted by any state agency to implement, interpret or make specific the law enforced or administered by it (Figure 2.3). In addition, the regulatory process is a formal process based on specified policies, principles and associated criteria and follows specified procedures as established in the management system. A firm must conduct its business with due skill, care and diligence. A firm must take reasonable care to organize and control its affairs responsibly and effectively, with adequate risk management systems. A firm must maintain adequate financial resources. A firm must observe proper standards of market conduct.

Likewise, the Risk Management Framework is a template and guideline used by companies to identify, eliminate and minimize risks. It was originally developed by the National Institute of Standards and Technology to help protect the information systems of the United States government.

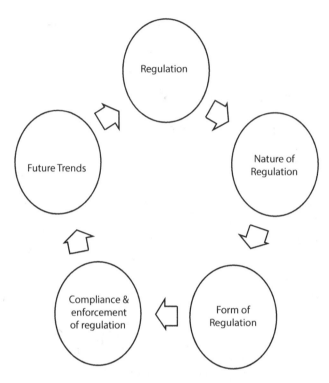

FIGURE 2.4
Proper standards of market conduct.

Risk Management Framework: Step by Step

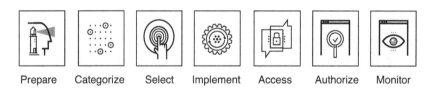

Prepare   Categorize   Select   Implement   Access   Authorize   Monitor

FIGURE 2.5
General idea of risk management.

Whereas cloud risk management is the process of assessing, securing and managing all kinds of risks related to cloud computing (Figure 2.4). It includes assessment across your organization's cloud footprint. Cloud storage risks include misconfiguration, data breaches, insecure interfaces, DDoS attacks, malware, insider threats, encryption issues and patching issues. Fortunately, there are mitigation strategies available to address each risk (Figure 2.5). Data risk management includes all practices for identifying risks, assessing risks and reducing risks to an acceptable level. This has always been important, but now the stakes are higher with new remote work, cybersecurity breaches and cloud security risks. Furthermore, the goal of a cloud risk assessment is to ensure that the system and data that exists in or is considered for migration to the cloud don't introduce any new or unidentified risks into the organization. Managing risks in SaaS entails identifying, assessing and mitigating potential threats linked with software as a service (SaaS) applications. SaaS risk management protects sensitive data in cloud apps, preventing breaches and unauthorized access and ensuring data security. A cloud security risk assessment is an analysis of an organization's cloud infrastructure to determine its security posture. This is a critical process for any organization operating out of the cloud to better understand present risks and determine gaps in security coverage. One of the most significant risks associated with cloud security is the potential for a data breach. Hackers can gain access to cloud-based systems and steal sensitive information, such as financial data, personal information or intellectual property. Risk mitigation strategies and preventive plans are set out to minimize the probability of negative risks and enhance opportunities. The security controls are implemented in the cloud system and are assessed by proper assessment procedures to determine if security controls are effective to produce the desired outcome. Human error and misconfigurations are one of the leading causes of data loss in cloud computing, including mistakes such as accidentally deleting important files, misconfiguring settings, failing to back up correctly or not backing up version data. In the cloud, compliance can also become an issue when data is exposed to employees who are not supposed to have access to it, as well as when data is moved into the cloud without an appropriate permissions structure. The most reputable cloud providers encrypt all data to avoid potential security threats. This structured methodology allows organizations to assess, prioritize and remediate gaps in their data security, privacy and operations program.

AI risk management is the process of systematically identifying, mitigating and addressing the potential risks associated with AI technologies. This involves implementing data collection and storage protocols, access controls and bias detection techniques. High-quality data is essential for building trustworthy AI systems, and strong data governance helps mitigate risks associated with biased or compromised data. Furthermore, an effective AI risk assessment constitutes a thorough and rigorous process where all AI models, systems and capabilities deployed within an organization are evaluated to identify and mitigate any potential risks across different domains, such as security, privacy, fairness and accountability. In risk management, AI/ML has become synonymous with improving efficiency and productivity while reducing costs. This has been possible due to the technologies' ability to handle and analyze large volumes of unstructured data at faster speeds with considerably lower degrees of human intervention. A combined approach to AI risk mitigation combined approaches of technical and socio-technical tools are needed, depending on the use case, organization and its resources know-how, financial and product. An AI system is considered high-risk if it is used as a safety component of a product, or if it is a product itself that is covered by EU legislation. These systems must undergo a third-party assessment before they can be sold or used. Top companies in the AI Model Risk Management Industry, such as Microsoft (US), IBM (US) and SAS Institute (US). The global AI Model Risk management market is projected to register a CAGR of 12.9 percent during the forecast period, reaching USD 10.5 billion by 2029 from an estimated USD 5.7 billion in 2024. The first step in an AI risk assessment is to identify and rank the risks as unacceptable or prohibited, high, limited or minimal. If an organization identifies a risk as unacceptable, it will need to stop engaging in that AI processing activity, depending on applicable laws. AI is used in risk management in banking by analyzing large amounts of data to identify patterns and anomalies that indicate potential dangers, helping companies proactively detect and mitigate them. The advantages range from streamlining to saving time, eliminating biases and automating repetitive tasks, just to name a few. The disadvantages are things like costly implementation, potential human job loss and lack of emotion and creativity. For instance, by analyzing large sets of data, companies can proactively identify and assess potential risks before they escalate. That data can also be used to make informed decisions that will safeguard operations, reputation and bottom line. Credit risk management is the practice of mitigating losses by assessing a borrower's credit risk, including payment behavior and affordability. Data risk management includes all practices for identifying risks, assessing risks and reducing risks to an acceptable level. This has always been important, but now the stakes are higher with new remote work, cybersecurity breaches and cloud security. However, without timely and reliable data, risk management is unable to effectively manage uncertainties and support top-management decision-making. Using data takes the guesswork out of managing risk-related issues.

Big data management is the organization, administration and governance of large volumes of both structured and unstructured data. The goal of big data management is to ensure a high level of data quality and accessibility for business intelligence and big data analytics applications. Furthermore, strategic risk management is the process of recognizing risks, identifying their causes and effects and taking the relevant actions to mitigate them. Risks arise from inside and outside factors such as manufacturing failures, economic changes, shifts in consumer tastes, etc. Default risk refers to the likelihood that a borrower won't be able to make their required debt payments to a lender. The default risk posed by consumers can be gauged through their credit reports and credit scores. However, risk management techniques are systematic approaches or methods used to identify, assess and mitigate risks associated with various activities, processes or business decisions. These techniques minimize potential losses and maximize opportunities while ensuring safety, compliance and operational efficiency. There are five basic steps that are taken in the risk management process: identifying risks, analyzing risks, prioritizing the risks, implementing a solution and finally, the risk is monitored. Blockchain technology's advanced cryptographic techniques, which ensure the integrity and confidentiality of data transactions, are foundational to establishing resilience against risks that third-party interactions often pose. A variety of financial risks need to be considered while designing such blockchain applications, platforms and infrastructure, such as potential for financial loss, transaction settlement finality, consortium funding-related risks and intellectual property protection issues. The data is stored on multiple devices, or nodes, which are connected to the blockchain network. This distributed network of nodes helps to ensure that the data is secure, as it is not stored in a single point of failure and is resistant to tampering. Data is sensitive and crucial, and blockchain can significantly change how we view critical information. By creating a record that can't be altered and is encrypted end-to-end, the blockchain helps prevent fraud and unauthorized activity.

Blockchain vendors face their own issues, including partner hesitation, lack of network effect, limited skills and financial issues. Among the technical challenges are performance and limited interoperability with the necessary systems. However, blockchain networks and the members of the blockchain, including nodes, are vulnerable to certain types of cyberattacks. The most common attack vectors are 51 percent Routing, Phishing scams and Sybil attacks. One crucial ethical implication of blockchain technology is the level of data security and privacy protection it provides. Health data is encrypted and shared within a network of known users where each data access and transfer can be traced. It utilizes powerful cryptography to give individuals ownership of an address, and the cryptoassets associated with it, through a combination of public and private keys, made up of combinations of random numbers and letters. Blockchain networks are designed differently in that the logs of the transactions with the data set are used to formulate the world state of the data. The use of cryptographic authentication of time-stamped blocks of transactions allows the entire network the benefit of certainty of the entire transactional history. However, smart contract bugs, consensus mechanism flaws, and cryptographic weaknesses pose significant security risks. Hackers may exploit vulnerabilities in blockchain networks to launch various attacks, including 51 percent attacks, double-spending attacks and distributed denial-of-service (DDoS) attacks.

Finally, it includes risks associated with poor quality control, employee error, theft, fraud, data loss, cyberattacks, natural disasters and regulatory compliance issues. All the elements in the regulatory reporting process, such as preparation, review and reports, are associated with operational risk.

3

Legal Guardianship

Navigating Data Regulations and Threat Landscapes

3.1 Overview of Relevant Laws and Regulations (GDPR, CCPA, etc.)

GDPR is an EU law with mandatory rules for how organizations and companies must use personal data in an integrity-friendly way. Personal data means any information which could directly or indirectly identify a living person. Name, phone number, and address are textbook examples of personal data. The GDPR protects data subjects, defined as "an identified or identifiable natural person," whereas the CCPA gives certain rights to consumers, defined as "a natural person who is a California resident." The GDPR applies to the processing of personal data by automated means or non-automated means if the data is part of a filing system. The CCPA does not specifically delineate a material scope, but its obligations cover "collecting," "selling" or "sharing" personal information. GDPR regulation guidelines are:

- Requiring the consent of subjects for data processing.
- Anonymizing collected data to protect privacy.
- Providing data breach notifications.
- Safely handling the transfer of data across borders.

The key components of GDPR are:

- fair and lawful processing.
- purpose limitation.
- data minimization and data retention.

Data security is the process of safeguarding digital information throughout its entire life cycle to protect it from corruption, theft or unauthorized

DOI: 10.1201/9781003604679-3

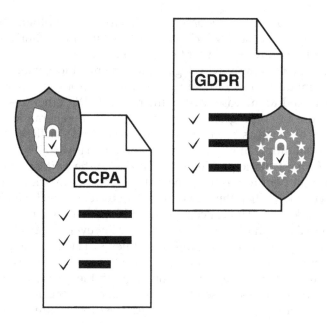

FIGURE 3.1
Relevant laws of data protection.

access. It covers everything such as hardware, software, storage devices and user devices; access and administrative controls; and organization policies and procedures (Figure 3.1). A data security policy is a set of guidelines, rules and standards organizations establish to manage and protect their data assets. It provides a framework for ensuring that data is handled, stored, transmitted and accessed in a way that maintains its confidentiality, integrity and availability. Now since an Act to provide for data protection with due regard to the declaration of rights under the constitution and the public and national interest, to establish a Cyber Security Centre, a Data Protection Authority and to provide for their functions, to create a technology driven business environment. That provides legal recognition for electronic documents and a framework to support e-filing and e-commerce transactions, as well as a legal framework to mitigate cybercrimes.

Cybersecurity law sets out rules and guidelines for securing cyberspace and helps shape national security in a digital world. Coordination between organizations, public authorities, the private sector, government and even people helps to build a framework to follow. Data protection application can stop cyberattacks and protects from theft, including insider-led data loss. Data security such as cybersecurity resources that protect from unauthorized access and data manipulation or corruption. While it uses cybersecurity frameworks, assurance services and best practices to reduce risks against attacks and fraud. Blockchain technology produces a structure of data with inherent security qualities. It's based on principles of cryptography, decentralization and consensus, which ensure trust in transactions. After all, the GDPR is based on the assumption that data can be modified or erased where necessary to comply with legal requirements. Blockchains, however, render such modifications of data purposefully onerous in order to ensure data integrity and to increase trust in the network. With their decentralized design and use of cryptography, blockchains are, in general, fairly secure. Once a block of data has been added to the chain and verified, it cannot be removed, and multiple blocks are always stored linearly. So it's easy to check the ledger for systematic problems. When one of the participants needs to add a new data item to the blockchain, they first symmetrically encrypt it using the secret key. Then the transaction with the encrypted data is submitted to the blockchain. The concepts behind blockchain technology make it nearly impossible to hack into a blockchain. However, weaknesses outside of the blockchain create opportunities for thieves. Hackers can gain access to cryptocurrency owners' cryptocurrency wallets, exchange accounts or the exchanges themselves. Like other technology-enabled systems, blockchain systems also need to be assessed for a variety of cybersecurity risks, such as confidentiality of users, security of private keys that secure access to digital assets and endpoint protection. As all transactions are recorded across all nodes, hackers cannot steal, hack or tamper with data unless a platform-level vulnerability exists.

It is necessary to need CGPA for schools and colleges. CGPA is used to measure the overall academic achievement of a student by awarding A, B, C, D or F grades. CGPA is a calculation of the average grade point obtained in all subjects except in additional subjects as per the study scheme. Hence, the difference between CGPA and GDPR is that GDPR requires explicit and freely given consent, whereas PDPA allows for implied consent in certain circumstances. Additionally, GDPR introduces additional legal bases for processing personal data, such as legitimate interests and contractual necessity, while PDPA primarily relies on consent and other exceptions. However, the GDPR does not apply if: the data subject is dead; the data subject is a legal person; the processing is done by a person acting for purposes which are outside his trade, business or profession. Furthermore, the aim of GDPR is to protect individuals when their data is being processed by the private sector and most of the public sector.

The CCPA gives Californians several basic rights: the right to know what personal information is being collected about them, the right to access that data, the right to know who it's being sold to and the right to opt out of those sales. Finally, the EEA GDPR applies to all 27 member countries of the European Union (EU). It also applies to all countries in the European Economic Area (the EEA). The EEA is an area larger than the EU and includes Iceland, Norway and Liechtenstein.

3.2 Compliance Requirements for Different Industries

There are two main types of compliance that denote where the framework is coming from: corporate and regulatory. Both corporate and regulatory compliance consist of a framework of rules, regulations and practices to follow.

External compliance, also known as regulatory compliance, refers to following the rules, regulations and industry standards set by the law. These are mandatory guidelines you must follow in order to stay in business. For example, registering your business name is an act of practicing external compliance. However, regulatory compliance is the process of complying with applicable laws, regulations, policies and procedures, standards and the other rules issued by governments and regulatory bodies like FINRA, SEC, FDA, NERC, Financial Conduct Authority (FCA), etc. A compliance standard is an Enterprise Manager's representation of a compliance control that must be tested against a set of IT infrastructure to determine whether the control is being followed. Incidentally, the five Cs of compliance are: calm, credible, clear, confident and courageous. Compliance leadership keeps management, the board and employees calm to manage crises and keep defenses strong to remain diligent against harm, including fraud, misconduct and criminal activity (Figure 3.2). Furthermore, the global template organizes key enforcement and regulatory issues into five essential compliance program elements: leadership, risk assessment, standards and controls, training and communication and oversight. The policies and procedures should be dynamic, not static. Presentation, placement, proximity and prominence are four measurements used to ensure that all marketing materials meet federal and state compliance requirements. Industry compliance means that a company adheres to the applicable rules and laws. This includes both country-specific laws and requirements from the regulatory authorities, as well as internal company directives. A range of tools and process can be implemented by a company to bring about good compliance. There are eight steps to ensuring regulatory compliance:

- Determine which regulations are relevant to your business.
- Identify the specific requirements you need to comply with.
- Conduct an initial internal audit.
- Establish and document compliance policies and procedures.
- Provide your employees with regular compliance training.
- Rely on experts.
- Constantly improve your regulatory compliance.
- Leverage tech tools and entrust the right software providers.

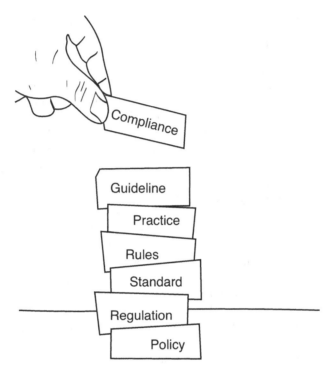

FIGURE 3.2
Compliance requirements for different industries.

Statutory requirements—Laws passed by a state or central government. Regulatory Requirements—A rule issued by a regulatory body appointed by a state and/or central government.

Standard—Documented procedure whose intention is to harmonize actions or processes within a specific discipline or activity.

Cyber-compliance refers to the process of ensuring that an organization adheres to industry regulations, standards and laws related to information security and data privacy. Many different types of organizations may need to comply with various cybersecurity regulations and standards. The differences between regulatory compliance and compliance are: Regulatory compliance follows legal mandates, essentially a framework of rules, regulations and practices to be adhered to. Corporate compliance refers to a company following rules and regulations mandated by certain governing bodies, as well as their own internal compliance structure.

ISO compliance is achieved when an organization meets the requirements outlined in a specific standard developed by the International Organization for Standardization (ISO). ISO has developed thousands of standards that cover all areas of business. Most commonly, they start with SOC 2 or ISO 27001. These two standards benefit from broad recognition. They establish a baseline of information security and compliance practices that lays a good

FIGURE 3.3
Regulatory compliance vs. corporate compliance.

foundation for working with enterprise customers and the other compliance standards on the list (Figure 3.3). However, the three main pillars of compliance: People, Process, and Technology: The Three Pillars of Effective Compliance Management. Organizational exposure to compliance risk is increasing consistently while compliance costs are skyrocketing. A reactive approach to compliance creates complexity and forces organizations to be less agile. The three Rs of compliance are: reputation, reciprocity and retaliation. They are the keys to understanding why states comply with international obligations. Compliance plans allow for the creation of an overall plan to address regulatory requirements in a structured setting, or to structure a set of regulatory tasks. For example, a compliance plan might be created to track regulatory tasks, or to conduct compliance assessments against various regulatory requirements. The elements of compliance are:

- Implementing written policies and procedures.
- All policies can be found in the Policy Library.
- Effective lines of communication.
- Various methods to report via the Hotline.
- Internal auditing and monitoring.
- Enforcement and disciplinary guidelines.
- Prompt response.

FIGURE 3.4a
Seven elements for chief compliance officers.

FIGURE 3.4b
Compliance testing.

Compliance key performance indicators, or KPIs, are metrics that help you measure how successful your compliance performance is in relation to your strategic goals (Figure 3.4a). These include how compliant your organization is in its internal and external policies, as well as in terms of the regulatory landscape in which you work. The Global Regulatory Compliance market size was valued at USD 17135.97 million in 2022 and is expected to expand at a CAGR of 6.03 percent during the forecast period, reaching USD 24348.16 million by 2028. A compliance audit is an assessment of whether the provisions of the applicable laws, rules and regulations made there under and various orders and instructions issued by the competent authority are being complied with (Figure 3.4b). A certificate of compliance is a document that certifies that a product or system meets the requirements of a safety regulation or standard. It is typically used in shipping and logistics to ensure that products are safe for transport and meet the destination country's requirements. Compliance documentation consists of "specific records and reports of information required to verify the implementation of a compliance program." To simplify, it is a record of what type of compliance program you have in place and what the program includes. Consequently, compliance testing, in its most basic form, is testing software to ensure it meets specified regulatory and industry requirements. These regulations address various topics, including security, accessibility, and data privacy.

A cybersecurity standard is a set of guidelines or best practices that organizations can use to improve their cybersecurity posture. Organizations can use cybersecurity standards to help them identify and implement appropriate measures to protect their systems and data from cyber threats. ISO 27001 and ISO 27002 are two of the most common standards for information security management today. These standards provide a comprehensive framework for organizations looking to protect their data through robust policies and best practices. Cybersecurity is the practice of defending computers, servers, mobile devices, electronic systems, networks and data from malicious attacks. It's also known as information technology security or electronic information security. NIST develops cybersecurity standards, guidelines, best practices and other resources to meet the needs of U.S. industries, federal agencies and the broader public. Cybersecurity governance is a comprehensive cybersecurity strategy that integrates with organizational operations and prevents the interruption of activities due to cyber threats or attacks. Features of cybersecurity governance include accountability frameworks as well as decision-making hierarchies. The IEEE Cybersecurity Standards collection offers access to standards in the cybersecurity technology area designed to help improve the quality of exchange framework, cryptographic assets, data authentication, e-commerce and Internet of Things (IoT). The MCSS (Minimum Cyber Security Standard) sets out a series of mandatory cyber-resilience outcomes that all government departments must achieve to meet their obligations under the Security Policy Framework and

National Cyber Security Strategy. Web security standards specify coding standards and basic security practices that must be followed when developing and improving websites and web applications. The OWASP Application Security Checklist is a list of key items to review and verify effectiveness. Common cybersecurity standards include ISO 27001, PCI DSS and the NIST cybersecurity framework. These standards provide a set of best practices for managing and mitigating cyber-risks and are widely used by organizations across various industries. A cybersecurity standard defines both functional and assurance requirements within a product, system, process or technology environment. Well-developed cybersecurity standards enable consistency among product developers and serve as a reliable metric for purchasing security products. It involves verifying that nobody uses AI-powered systems to invade individuals' privacy or cause any harm to them. AI compliance also ensures that AI-powered systems are employed responsibly and in a way that benefits society. A real-world example that is quite common today is a website development company that might mandate that all websites must be responsive.

Industry standards or rules set outside an organization are external standards. For example, a health care company may require that all software it develops must be HIPAA-compliant. AI plays a crucial role in risk management within compliance. It can predict potential compliance risks and suggest measures to mitigate them. AI systems can monitor real-time transactions, providing alerts on suspicious activities that may indicate non-compliance or fraud. Furthermore, AI compliance is crucial for several reasons. It ensures the ethical use of technology, mitigates risks associated with legal consequences, fosters consumer trust, protects data privacy, promotes innovation and adoption, enforces transparency and accountability and meets legal requirements in various jurisdictions.

A fundamental challenge in deploying AI compliance management systems is ensuring the quality and integrity of the data these systems rely on. High-quality data is essential for AI to function effectively, as even the most advanced algorithms can produce poor outcomes if the underlying data is inaccurate or incomplete. However, compliance testing allows us to check that the company is following the protocols established in providing services to maintain the same levels on all output and help earn the trust of clientele. This can help to perform quality control measures successfully. AI, particularly NLP, is utilized in auditing to analyze large volumes of textual data. Auditors often have to review contracts, emails and other textual information for compliance and risk assessment, and NLP algorithms can extract relevant information, identify key terms and assess the sentiment or tone of the text. The regulation of artificial intelligences is the development of public sector policies and laws for promoting and regulating AI. Regulation is now generally considered necessary to both encourage AI and manage associated risks. AI is a valuable tool to streamline and support the compliance function. A compliance officer's role entails understanding that AI is not yet equipped to replicate. Educational tools powered by AI could make compliance knowledge more accessible. AI-generated solutions require human oversight for validation.

Blockchain compliance refers to the adherence of blockchain technology and its applications to relevant laws, regulations and industry standards within a legal context. It involves making sure that all parts of the blockchain, like transactions and smart contracts, function as they should. The goal is to find and fix any problems before the system is used in the real world. This helps ensure the blockchain is reliable, safe from attacks and performs well under different conditions. The major areas to focus on while testing include the block size, chain size, data transmission capabilities and addition of a new block. Ensure data integrity so that there is no loss of information in the blockchain application. Test small units first, then switch to end-to-end testing. Compliance plays a key role in legitimizing and stabilizing cryptocurrency markets around the world. Based on recent violations, it's clear that the major compliance areas include Anti-Money Laundering (AML), Know Your Customer (KYC) and adherence to international sanctions. Important processes in crypto-compliance include risk assessment, continuous feedback and monitoring, updates in policies according to regulations and KYC or KYB processes. Now that crypto-asset trading companies must augment traditional AML procedures to include crypto-specific tracking and analysis in their compliance regimens, including using blockchain intelligence tools to identify risky or terrorist-associated crypto-wallet addresses Cryptocurrency regulations across jurisdictions can range from detailed rules designed to support blockchain users to outright bans on the trading or use of cryptocurrencies. Digital asset regulations may address how digital money is created, bought, sold and traded.

Furthermore, process compliance is the regulation and maintenance of industry standards and guidelines. Most industries have standards and guidelines relating to the execution of their business processes. Some of these are actual laws, and non-compliance can result in stiff penalties or even jail time for company officers. A good compliance program should include policies and procedures that are regularly reviewed and updated as necessary. The program should also include training and education for employees to ensure that they understand their responsibilities and the regulations they must follow. Likewise, the main difference between non-statutory and statutory bodies is that statutory bodies are created by an act of parliament, while non-statutory bodies are not. Statutory bodies have legal powers and are binding, while non-statutory bodies do not have any legal powers and are only advisory. A compliance framework is a structured set of guidelines that details an organization's processes for maintaining accordance with established regulations, specifications or legislation. Compliance management is the ongoing process of monitoring and assessing systems to ensure they comply with industry and security standards, as well as corporate and regulatory policies and requirements.

ISO 9001 is defined as the international standard that specifies requirements for a quality management system (QMS). Organizations use the standard to demonstrate their ability to consistently provide products and services that meet customer and regulatory requirements. ISO 9001 provides an audit checklist that organizations are required to use when conducting internal audits. The checklist includes questions for assessing an organization's context, leadership, planning and quality management systems, support structures, operations, performance evaluation and areas for improvement. People often say "ISO Certified," but ISO does not issue certificates or certify individual companies to any standard. They are issued by certification or registration bodies (also called Registrars or CBs), which are independent of ISO.

Cloud compliance refers to the process of adhering to regulatory standards, international laws and mandates and industry best practices, such as frameworks and benchmarks in the context of cloud computing. It ensures that cloud services and the data they handle meet specific security, privacy and operational criteria. Process compliance is the regulation and maintenance of industry standards and guidelines. Most industries have standards and guidelines relating to the execution of their business processes. Some of these are actual laws, and non-compliance can result in stiff penalties or even jail time for company officers. Cloud computing relies heavily on virtualization and automation technologies (Figure 3.5). Virtualization lets IT organizations create virtual instances of servers, storage and other resources that let multiple VMs or cloud environments run on a single physical server using software known as a hypervisor. Cloud compliance consists of the procedures and practices that ensure that a cloud environment complies with governance rules. In other words, when you build a compliant cloud environment, the environment conforms to one or more specific sets of security and privacy standards. Cloud security staying compliant involves implementing stringent access controls, encryption protocols and regular security audits to safeguard against unauthorized access and data breaches. So need to meet various standards to show how can protect data. AWS compliance empowers customers to understand the robust controls in place at AWS to maintain security and data protection in the AWS Cloud. When systems are built in the AWS Cloud, AWS and customers share compliance responsibilities. However, cloud compliance refers to the process of ensuring that an organization's use of cloud-based services, resources and technologies adheres to relevant laws and regulations governing data privacy, security and management. Achieving cloud compliance helps organizations mitigate risks and protect sensitive information. Furthermore, blockchain compliance refers to the adherence of blockchain technology and its applications to relevant laws, regulations and industry standards within a legal context. Blockchain uses the three principles of cryptography, decentralization and consensus to create a highly secure underlying software system that is nearly impossible to

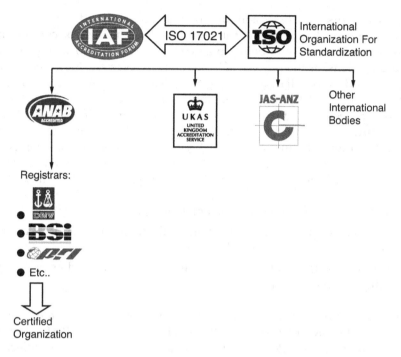

FIGURE 3.5
The process of compliance.

tamper with. There is no single point of failure, and a single user cannot change the transaction records.

Nodes are the base of the blockchain. A node is a miner that connects to the Bitcoin (BSV) network to find blocks and process transactions. Nodes communicate with each other by transmitting information within the distributed system using the Bitcoin peer-to-peer protocol. All the transactions within the blockchain are recorded in a transparent manner to an absolute ledger with a secure authentication process, and more efficient and rapid asset-tracing can take place than is currently the norm. Important processes in crypto-compliance include risk assessment, continuous feedback and monitoring, updates in policies according to regulations and KYC or KYB processes. Workflows are used to guide users from independent organizations to process and manage transactions, data and documents in a trusted, immutable and transparent manner for all relevant entities on a given blockchain network.

Big data governance refers to the framework of policies, procedures and standards that ensure the proper management of data assets. It involves the coordination of people, processes and technology to achieve high data quality, maintain data security and ensure regulatory compliance. Data compliance is the formal governance structure in place to ensure an organization complies with laws, regulations and standards around its data. The process governs the possession, organization, storage and management of digital assets or data to prevent it from loss, theft, misuse or compromise. Compliance is the state of being in accordance with established guidelines or specifications, or the process of becoming so. Software, for example, may be developed in compliance with specifications created by a standards body and then deployed by user organizations in compliance with a vendor's licensing agreement. At its core, cybersecurity compliance means adhering to standards and regulatory requirements set forth by some agency, law or authority group. Organizations must achieve compliance by establishing risk-based controls that protect the confidentiality, integrity and availability (CIA) of information. The compliance process typically involves these steps:

- Risk assessment to identify potential areas of risk.
- Compliance program development and implementation to address these risks.
- Communication and training to ensure employees understand and adhere to the program.

Common cybersecurity compliance regulations include the General Data Protection Regulation (GDPR), the Health Insurance Portability and Accountability Act (HIPAA) and the Payment Card Industry Data Security Standard (PCI DSS). Compliance and security are two sides of the same coin. While security measures are driven by business risk, compliance is fueled by legal obligation and demonstrates to clients that they can trust your organization to keep their data free from harm.

Whether the cloud service providers SOC 2 compliance is crucial for cloud providers, given how much sensitive customer data they handle:

- Data centers.
- Financial services.
- Healthcare service providers.
- Third-party SaaS vendors.
- Any company that values data security.

Compliance criteria means all terms, conditions, instructions, concentration limits and maximum permissible values listed or specified in the Environmental Compliance Certificate, as well as in all laws including all policies and guidelines having the force of law, which have been or will be issued by a Governmental site. Finally, compliance metrics are quantifiable measures of how well a company's compliance team performs. By assessing information like total incidents, the time between issues, key risk indicators and compliance cost, compliance teams can recognize areas for improvement and capitalize on their strengths.

3.3 Case Studies of Legal Consequences for Data Breaches

3.3.1 Equifax Data Breach—Expired Certificates
Delayed Breach Detection

In the spring of 2017, the U.S. Department of Homeland Security's Computer Emergency Readiness Team (CERT) sent consumer credit reporting agency Equifax a notice about a vulnerability affecting certain versions of Apache Struts. According to former CEO Richard Smith, Equifax sent out a mass internal email about the flaw. The company's IT security team should have used this email to fix the vulnerability, according to Smith's testimony before the House Energy and Commerce Committee. But that didn't happen. An automatic scan several days later also failed to identify the vulnerable version of Apache Struts. Plus, the device inspecting encrypted traffic was misconfigured because of a digital certificate that had expired ten months previously. Together, these oversights enabled a digital attacker to crack into Equifax's system in mid-May and maintain their access until the end of July.

> **How encryption may become a factor in scenarios like this:** Once attackers have access to a network, they can install rogue or stolen certificates that allow them to hide exfiltration in encrypted traffic. Unless HTTPS inspection solutions are available and have full access to all keys and certificates, rogue certificates will remain undetected.

> **Impact:** The bad actor is thought to have exposed the personal information of 145 million people in the United States and more than 10 million UK citizens. In September 2018, the Information Commissioner's Office issued Equifax a fine of £500,000, the maximum penalty amount allowed under the Data Protection Act 1998, for failing to protect the personal information of up to 15 million UK citizens during the data breach.

3.3.2 Ericsson Data Breach—Mobile Services Go
Dark When the Certificate Expires

At the beginning of December 2018, a digital certificate used by Swedish multinational networking and telecommunications company Ericsson for its SGSN–MME (Serving GPRS Support Node— Mobility Management Entity) software expired. This incident caused outages for customers of various UK mobile carriers including O2, GiffGaff, and Lyca Mobile. As a result, a total of 32 million people in the United Kingdom alone lost access to 4G and SMS on 6 December. Beyond the United Kingdom, the outage reached 11 countries including Japan.

> **How encryption may become a factor in scenarios like this:** Expired certificates do not only cause high-impact downtime; they can also leave critical systems without protection. If a security system

experiences a certificate outage, cybercriminals can take advantage of the temporary lack of availability to bypass the safeguards.

Impact: Ericsson restored the most affected customer services over the course of 6 December. The company also noted in a blog post that "The faulty software for two versions of SGSN–MME that has caused these issues is being decommissioned."

3.3.3 Strathmore College Data Breach—Student Records Not Adequately Protected

In August 2018, it appears that an employee at Strathmore Secondary College accidentally published more than 300 students' records on the school's intranet. These records included students' medical and mental health conditions such as Asperger's, autism and ADHD. According to The Guardian, they also listed the exposed students' medications along with any learning and behavioral difficulties. Overall, the records remained on Strathmore's intranet for about a day. During that time, students and parents could have viewed and or downloaded the information.

How encryption may become a factor in scenarios like this: Encrypting access to student records makes it difficult for anyone who doesn't have the proper credentials to access them. Any information left unprotected by encryption can be accessed by any cybercriminals who penetrate the perimeter.

Impact: Strathmore's principal had arranged professional development training for staff to ensure they were following best security practices. Meanwhile, Australia's Department of Education announced that it would investigate what had caused the breach.

3.3.4 Marine Corps Data Breach—Unencrypted Email Misfires

At the beginning of 2018, the Defense Travel System (DTS) of the United States Department of Defense (DOD) sent out an unencrypted email with an attachment to the wrong distribution list. The email, which the DTS sent within the usmc.mil official unclassified Marine domain but also to some civilian accounts, exposed the personal information of approximately 21,500 Marines, sailors and civilians. Per Marine Corp Times, the data included victims' bank account numbers, truncated Social Security Numbers and emergency contact information.

How encryption may become a factor in scenarios like this: If organizations are not using proper encryption, cybercriminals can insert themselves between two email servers to intercept and read the email.

Sending private personal identity information over unencrypted channels essentially becomes an open invitation to cybercriminals.

Impact: Upon learning of the breach, the Marines implemented email recall procedures to limit the number of email accounts that would receive the email. They also expressed their intention to implement additional security measures going forward.

3.3.5 Pennsylvania Department of Education Data Breach—Misassigned Permissions

In February 2018, an employee in Pennsylvania's Office of Administration committed an error that subsequently affected the state's Teacher Information Management System (TIMS). As reported by PennLive, the incident temporarily enabled individuals who logged into TIMS to access personal information belonging to other users including teachers, school districts and Department of Education staff. In all, the security event is believed to have affected as many as 360,000 current and retired teachers.

How encryption may become a factor in scenarios like this: If you do not know who's accessing an organization's information, then you will never know if it's being accessed by cybercriminals. Encrypting access to vital information and carefully managing the identities of the machines that house it will help you control access.

Impact: Pennsylvania's Department of Education subsequently sent out notice letters informing victims that the incident might have exposed their personal information including their Social Security Numbers. It also offered a free one-year subscription for credit monitoring and identity protection services to affected individuals.

Since the regulations like HIPAA, GDPR and CCPA allow authorities to issue hefty fines for failing to properly secure data or not disclosing breaches in a timely manner. State laws also allow customers to sue for damages. Class-action lawsuits following large breaches have cost companies hundreds of millions of dollars. Data breaches can affect the brand's reputation and cause the company to lose customers. Breaches can damage and corrupt databases. Data breaches can also have legal and compliance consequences. They can also significantly impact individuals, causing loss of privacy and, in some cases, identity theft. Finally, all 50 states, the District of Columbia, Guam, Puerto Rico and the U.S. Virgin Islands have established data breach laws to protect consumers. These laws generally require organizations to notify individuals in the case of a data breach involving certain personal identifying information.

3.4 Threat Landscape

The threat landscape means the entire scope of potential and recognized cybersecurity threats affecting user groups, organizations, specific industries or a particular time. The term "Cyber Threat Landscape" describes the broad picture that represents potential cybersecurity risks and identified threats faced by individuals, organizations and societies in the internet world. It covers the numerous risks, weaknesses, and actors that are present in the cybersecurity field. After all, an organization's attack surface is the sum of vulnerabilities, pathways or methods—sometimes called attack vectors—that hackers can use to gain unauthorized access to the network or sensitive data, or to carry out a cyberattack. Consequently, as security leaders know, the threat landscape is constantly changing. As technology develops at rapid rates, so do common cyberattack methods. The explosion of artificial intelligence has made it easier for cybercriminals to launch attacks with fewer resources or skills. Furthermore, expect cybercriminals to leverage AI and ML to automate and enhance their capabilities, making attacks more sophisticated and adaptive. Cybersecurity professionals must harness the power of AI themselves to stay one step ahead of these evolving threats.

The digital landscape is constantly evolving, and with it, so are the threats faced by organizations of all sizes. For enterprises, the stakes are high—securing sensitive data, protecting critical infrastructure and maintaining operational continuity are paramount. Cybersecurity attacks use attack vectors to gain unauthorized access to a system or network. The attack surface is the number of attack vectors a cybercriminal can access. The 2024 Global Threat Report unveils an alarming rise in covert activity and a cyber threat landscape dominated by stealth. Data theft, cloud breaches, and malware-free attacks are on the rise. Furthermore, types of cyber threats institutions should be aware of include:

- Malware.
- Ransomware.
- Distributed denial of service (DDoS) attacks.
- Spam and Phishing.
- Corporate Account Takeover (CATO)
- Automated Teller Machine (ATM) Cash Out.

When looking to the future, the ever-evolving landscape of cybersecurity means that new threats and attack methods are emerging constantly; therefore it is crucial for organizations and individuals alike to stay of these emerging threats in order to protect themselves and their systems. Likewise, to protect against the threat landscape, utilize methods such as:

- Implement strong access controls.
- Regularly update software and systems.
- Conduct regular employee training.
- Implement robust incident response plans.
- Use encryption and Data Loss Prevention (DLP).
- Conduct regular security assessments.
- Establish a supply chain security program.

Cybersecurity is the practice of protecting systems, networks and programs from digital attacks (Figure 3.6). These cyberattacks are usually aimed at accessing, changing or destroying sensitive information; extorting money from users via ransomware; or interrupting normal business processes.

The term "Cyber Threat Landscape" describes the broad picture that represents potential cybersecurity risks and identified threats faced by individuals, organizations and societies in the internet world. It covers the numerous risks, weaknesses and actors that are present in the cybersecurity field. Thus,

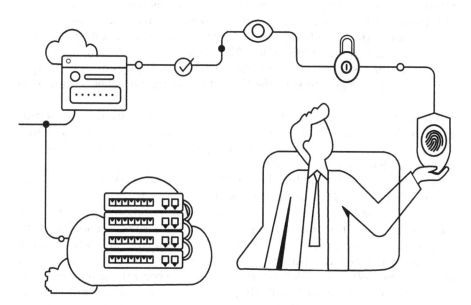

FIGURE 3.6
Cyber threat landscape.

web security is a set of procedures, practices and technologies for protecting web servers, web users and their surrounding organizations. Security protects you against unexpected behavior. As cybercriminals become increasingly sophisticated and cybersecurity threats continue to rise, organizations are becoming more and more aware of the potential threat posed by third parties. However, the risk is still high; U.S. Customs and Border Protection joined the list of high-profile victims in 2021. However, threat mitigation (also called cyber-risk mitigation or cyberattack mitigation) is a term that describes the tools, processes and strategies companies use to reduce the severity or seriousness of a potential data breach or other cyberattack. As a result, threat intelligence—also called "cyber threat intelligence" (CTI) or "threat intel"—is detailed, actionable threat information for preventing and fighting cybersecurity threats targeting an organization. For operating system hardening: Apply OS updates, service packs and patches automatically; remove unnecessary drivers, file sharing, libraries, software, services and functionality; encrypt local storage; tighten registry and other systems permissions; log all activity, errors and warnings; implement privileged users. Security threats, by definition, are any type of malicious activity or attack that could potentially cause harm or damage to an organization, its data or its personnel. Consequently, internet-based threats expose people and computer systems to harm online. A broad scope of dangers fits into this category, including well-known threats like phishing and computer viruses. However, other threats, like offline data theft, can also be considered part of this group. Furthermore, removable media devices have several notable consumer safety risks, including physical loss or theft, malware, data exfiltration and Autorun.in viruses. Physical loss/theft: These devices are small and easy to misplace or lose. For enhanced threat detection and prediction, companies are using AI algorithms to identify patterns and anomalies within large data sets.

A virus is a relatively small file that can copy itself into another file or program (its host). It can be transmitted only if its host file or program is transmitted. Some viruses are designed to change themselves slightly in order to make their detection and removal more difficult.

Cloud security offers reduced costs. With cloud security, you don't have to pay for dedicated hardware to upgrade your security or use valuable resources to handle security updates and configurations. CSPs provide advanced security features that offer automated protection capabilities with little to no human intervention. Finally, risk avoidance is the elimination of hazards, activities and exposures that can negatively affect an organization and its assets. Whereas risk management aims to control the damages and financial consequences of threatening events, risk avoidance seeks to avoid compromising events entirely.

4

Guarding against the Tide

Understanding and Countering Cyber Threats

4.1 Common Cyber Threats (Malware, Phishing, Ransomware, etc.)

Malware is the most common type of cyberattack, mostly because this term encompasses many subsets such as ransomware, trojans, spyware, viruses, worms, keyloggers, bots, cryptojacking and any other type of malware attack that leverages software in a malicious way. Hence, a cyber threat is an activity intended to compromise the security of an information system by altering its availability. Availability is applied to information assets, software and hardware (infrastructure and its components). Some examples of threats are:

- Rising material costs.
- Increasing competition.
- Tight labor supply.
- Failure to get approvals.
- Legal or regulatory issues.
- Supply chain breakdowns.
- Weather or natural disasters.

Threats can be classified into three primary categories: natural, technological and human-made. The biggest cybersecurity threats are phishing and social engineering. For several years now, these have been the most widespread and effective cyberattacks facing small businesses. Phishing, and its associated variants such as spear-phishing and business email compromise, is the most prevalent cyberthreat in the US. Cyberthreat class ten is any unauthorized act of gaining access to a computer network to disrupt processes or obtain data. Understand the definition of cyber threats, and discover types of cyber threats, such as trojans, worms, phishing and unpatched software. A vulnerability is a weakness or flaw in an operating system, network or

DOI: 10.1201/9781003604679-4

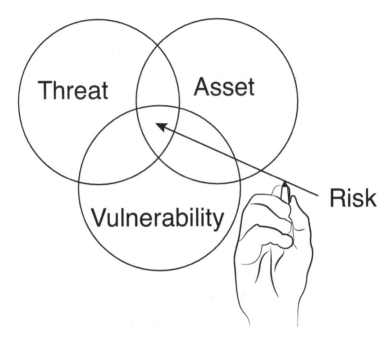

FIGURE 4.1
Common cyber threats.

application. A threat actor tries to exploit vulnerabilities to gain unauthorized access to data or systems (Figure 4.1). The security health page addresses many types of security threats—for example, malware, data exfiltration, data leaks and account breaches. Threats can be classified into four different categories; direct, indirect, veiled, conditional. A direct threat identifies a specific target and is delivered in a straightforward, clear and explicit manner. Since a threat is the potential for a threat agent to exploit a vulnerability, a risk is the potential for loss when the threat happens.

Threat actors, also known as cyberthreat actors or malicious actors, are individuals or groups who intentionally cause harm to digital devices or systems. With around 2,220 cyberattacks each day, that equates to over 800,000 attacks each year. A threat, in the context of computer security, refers to anything that has the potential to cause serious harm to a computer system. A threat may or may not happen, but it has the potential to cause serious damage. Threats can lead to attacks on computer systems, networks and more. Spyware is one of the most common threats to internet users. Once installed, it monitors internet activity, tracks login credentials and spies on sensitive information. The primary goal of spyware is usually to obtain credit card numbers, banking information and passwords. Another type is a worm. A worm is a type of malware or malicious software that can replicate rapidly and spread across devices within a network. As it spreads, a worm consumes bandwidth, overloading infected systems and making them unreliable or unavailable. Phishing is when attackers send scam emails (or text messages) that contain links to malicious websites. The websites may contain malware (such as ransomware) which can sabotage systems and organizations. An attack vector, or threat vector, is a way for attackers to enter a network or system. Common attack vectors include social engineering attacks, credential theft, vulnerability exploits and insufficient protection against insider threats.

4.2 Emerging Threats (AI-Driven Attacks, Insider Threats, etc.)

Emerging threats such as cyber-attacks, climate change, new weapons of mass destruction technologies, etc., bring new challenges to FEMA's response and recovery mission. In the realm of cybersecurity, emerging threats refer to new tactics, techniques and procedures (TTPs) that cybercriminals employ to exploit, disrupt or breach security systems. These threats constantly evolve, making them harder to predict and mitigate. One way to identify new risks is through "horizon scanning." This process involves examining external information to uncover potential opportunities and threats. This information can be used support strategic decision-making and business preparedness. As technology evolves, so do cybersecurity trends, with data breaches, ransomware attacks and hacks becoming increasingly commonplace. Users can elevate expertise by enrolling in security courses led by industry experts, empowering them with the knowledge and skills needed for comprehensive data protection.

These attacks exploit the advanced capabilities of artificial intelligence, particularly in natural language processing, to create sophisticated and convincing cyber threats. With the ability to generate highly realistic and personalized phishing emails, AI algorithms can trick even the most vigilant users. Consequently, AI has the potential to generate malware that could evade detection by current security filters, but only if it is trained on quality exploited data. There is a realistic possibility that highly capable states have repositories of malware that are large enough to effectively train an AI model for this purpose. Furthermore, these attacks will use AI to manipulate software dependency chains, leading developers to inadvertently introduce vulnerabilities into their applications. This tactic is expected to be part of a broader trend where AI is not just a tool for defense but a weapon in the attackers' arsenal.

At the forefront of AI's contribution to cybersecurity lies its unparalleled capacity for threat detection and rapid response. Unlike rule-based systems that struggle to keep pace with the evolving tactics of cybercriminals, AI employs machine learning algorithms to analyze vast datasets in real-time. However, the biggest threats of AI are:

- Automation-spurred job loss.
- Deepfakes.
- Privacy violations.
- Algorithmic bias caused by bad data.
- Socioeconomic inequality.
- Market volatility.
- Weapons automatization.
- Uncontrollable self-aware AI.

In the realm of cybersecurity, emerging threats refer to new tactics, techniques and procedures (TTPs) that cybercriminals employ to exploit, disrupt or breach security systems (Figure 4.2). These threats constantly evolve, making them harder to predict and mitigate. The latest technologies in cybersecurity include Artificial Intelligence (AI) and Machine Learning (ML),

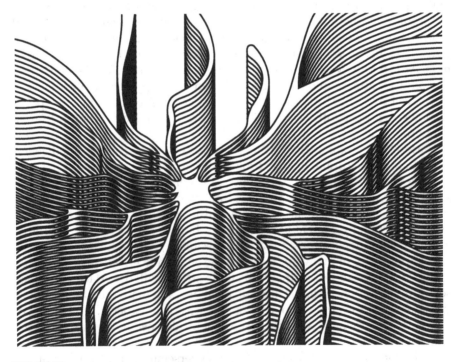

FIGURE 4.2
Emerging threats.

Behavioral Biometrics, Zero Trust Architecture, Blockchain, Quantum Computing, Cloud Security and IoT Security. Emerging technologies such as artificial intelligence, blockchain and the Internet of Things (IoT) are having a significant impact on cybersecurity. AI is being used to create more advanced and sophisticated cyber-attacks. Where supply chain compromise rise of digital surveillance authoritarianism or loss of privacy. Human error and exploited legacy systems within cyber-physical ecosystems. Now these emerging threats pose significant risks, such as financial losses, to businesses of all sizes. And advanced AI phishing attacks could lead to larger, more frequent financial fraud incidents. Data breaches' sophisticated impersonation techniques may trick employees into divulging sensitive information. There are myriad risks to do with AI that we deal with in our lives today. Not every AI risk is as big and worrisome as killer robots or sentient AI. Some of the biggest risks today include things like consumer privacy, biased programming, danger to humans and unclear legal regulation. AI can analyze past attacks and threat intelligence feeds to identify patterns and predict potential future attacks. This enables security teams to take preventative measures and bolster defenses before an attack even occurs. This proactive approach significantly enhances the overall security posture. After all, AI improves data processing tasks, from data collection and cleansing to transformation and storage. It reduces manual efforts and increases the speed and accuracy of data analytics. Predictive analytics powered by machine learning algorithms are used to forecast trends, customer behavior and market dynamics. Having access to a user's credentials and other sensitive information can result in losses for the user and the blockchain network. Blockchains rely on real-time, large data transfers. Hackers can intercept data as it's transferring to internet service providers. It is decentralized, meaning that it is not stored in any single location. Participants in the network confirm the transactions, or blocks, themselves so there is no need for a trusted third-party intermediary. Blockchain can have powerful applications in payments, supply chains and voting. However, blockchain technology introduces unique security challenges such as smart contract vulnerabilities, 51% attacks, phishing and social engineering attacks and insider threats. Like other technology-enabled systems, blockchain systems also need to be assessed for a variety of cybersecurity risks, such as confidentiality of users, security of private keys that secure access to digital assets and endpoint protection. An important challenge for blockchain networks is their energy consumption. These transactions consume huge amounts of energy. It is estimated that each Bitcoin transaction consumes 80,000 times more energy compared to a credit card transaction.

One of the primary concerns with big data is the potential for data privacy breaches and security vulnerabilities. Collecting and analyzing large volumes of data increases the risk of unauthorized access, data leaks and cyber-attacks, posing privacy and security risks for individuals and organizations. Artificial intelligence (AI) and machine learning (ML) are Big Data analytics trends. These technologies allow organizations to effectively process and analyze massive datasets, identify patterns and make accurate predictions. Big data is a combination of structured, semistructured and unstructured data that organizations collect, analyze and mine for information and insights. It's used in machine learning projects, predictive modeling and other advanced analytics applications. Big data is evolving with time and has increased its focus on artificial intelligence systems and machine learning to enhance and improve business processes. However, edge computing is considered to be the future after big data, as it supports and complements data processing via cloud integrations.

"AI-driven" refers to something that is powered or guided by artificial intelligence technologies. It implies that AI algorithms, systems or processes play a significant role in the functioning, decision-making or behavior of a particular product, service or system. These risks can manifest in various forms, including but not limited to data privacy breaches, biased outputs, AI hallucinations, deliberate attacks on AI systems and concentration of power in computer and data. In addition, awareness of these limitations is important for developers and organizations looking to deploy and use AI technology. Despite the significant progress AI and machine learning have made, these technologies are vulnerable to attacks that can cause spectacular failures with dire consequences. Likewise, an insider threat is a security risk that comes from within your company. Employees, partners, vendors, interns, suppliers or contractors can potentially become an insider threat. These people can access your organization's internal network and may accidentally leak or purposely steal sensitive information. In 2018, Facebook fired a security engineer accused of exploiting the privileged information his position accorded him to stalk women online. Also in 2018, a Tesla employee was alleged to have sabotaged company systems and sent proprietary information to third parties. Incidentally the intentional insider is often synonymously referenced as a "malicious insider." Intentional threats are actions taken to harm an organization for personal benefit or to act on a personal grievance. Furthermore, an accidental insider threat is the risk that someone who works for or with a company will make a mistake that potentially compromises the organization or its data or people. A negligent insider risk is when someone knowingly breaks a security policy but doesn't mean to cause harm. As a result, insider threats can pose a serious risk to a company's valuable data resources and intellectual property. The access and knowledge possessed by insiders can make them more dangerous to an organization than external threat actors.

4.3 Real-World Examples of Major Data Breaches and Their Impact

4.3.1 Yahoo

Date: August 2013

Impact: 3 billion accounts

Securing the number one spot—almost seven years after the initial breach and four since the true number of records exposed was revealed—is the attack on Yahoo. The company first publicly announced the incident—which it said took place in 2013—in December 2016. At the time, it was in the process of being acquired by Verizon and estimated that account information of more than a billion of its customers had been accessed by a hacking group. Less than a year later, Yahoo announced that the actual figure of user accounts exposed was 3 billion. Yahoo stated that the revised estimate did not represent a new "security issue" and that it was sending emails to all the "additional affected user accounts."

Despite the attack, the deal with Verizon was completed, albeit at a reduced price. Verizon's CISO Chandra McMahon said at the time:

> Verizon is committed to the highest standards of accountability and transparency, and we proactively work to ensure the safety and security of our users and networks in an evolving landscape of online threats. Our investment in Yahoo is allowing that team to continue to take significant steps to enhance their security, as well as benefit from Verizon's experience and resources.

After investigation, it was discovered that, while the attackers accessed account information such as security questions and answers, plaintext passwords, payment card and bank data were not stolen.

4.3.2 Alibaba

Date: November 2019

Impact: 1.1 billion pieces of user data

Over an eight-month period, a developer working for an affiliate marketer scraped customer data, including usernames and mobile numbers, from the Alibaba Chinese shopping website, Taobao, using crawler software that he created. It appears the developer and his employer were collecting the information for their own use and did not sell it on the black market, although both were sentenced to three years in prison.

A Taobao spokesperson said in a statement:

> Taobao devotes substantial resources to combat unauthorized scraping on our platform, as data privacy and security is of utmost importance. We have proactively discovered and addressed this unauthorized scraping. We will continue to work with law enforcement to defend and protect the interests of our users and partners.

4.3.3 Facebook

Date: April 2019

Impact: 533 million users

In April 2019, it was revealed that two datasets from Facebook apps had been exposed to the public internet. The information related to more than 530 million Facebook users and included phone numbers, account names and Facebook IDs. However, two years later (April 2021), the data was posted for free, indicating new and real criminal intent surrounding the data. In fact, given the sheer number of phone numbers impacted and readily available on the dark web as a result of the incident, security researcher Troy Hunt added functionality to his HaveIBeenPwned (HIBP) breached credential checking site that would allow users to verify if their phone numbers had been included in the exposed dataset.

Hunt wrote in a blog post:

> I'd never planned to make phone numbers searchable. My position on this was that it didn't make sense for a bunch of reasons. The Facebook data changed all that. There's over 500 million phone numbers but only a few million email addresses so >99% of people were getting a miss when they should have gotten a hit.

4.4 Data Protection Strategies

Most data protection strategies consist of three key focus areas:

- Data security—protecting data from malicious or accidental damage.
- Data availability—quickly restoring data in the event of damage or loss.
- Access control—ensuring that data is accessible to those who actually need it, and not to anyone else.

Encryption is a fundamental component for protecting personal data. It involves converting sensitive information into a coded form, making it unreadable to anyone without the proper decryption key. Only an authorized user who possesses the decryption key is able to decode and view the information. Some of the most common types of data security, which organizations should combine to ensure they have the best possible strategy, include encryption, data erasure, data masking and data resiliency. Data security controls encompass an array of cybersecurity measures taken to protect an organization's data. They include the mechanisms, procedures, policies and governance strategies to prevent and detect security incidents and data breaches. One example of data privacy is ensuring that sensitive data, such as financial information or medical records, is accessed only by authorized personnel. This can be achieved through access control measures, such as usernames and passwords, or biometric authentication. Encrypting data is another example of data privacy. The goal is to minimize the footprint of sensitive data and secure business-critical and regulated data. In particular, organizations use data protection strategies to prevent threat actors from gaining unauthorized access to data. Data level security is designed to prevent data corruption throughout its entire lifecycle. Further, data level security is a counterpart to privacy. The collection of data requires a straightforward security framework. ISO 27701 was developed to provide a standard for data privacy controls, which, when coupled with an ISMS, allows an organization to demonstrate effective privacy data management. It establishes the parameters for a PIMS in terms of privacy protection and processing personally identifiable information (PII). Consequently, data security is key to maintaining the confidentiality, integrity and availability of an organization's data. By implementing strong data security measures, organizations can help protect their valuable assets, meet relevant compliance requirements and maintain customer trust in the company's brand. Furthermore, the General Data Protection Regulation (GDPR) talks about protecting the privacy rights of data subjects (individuals) in the European Union (EU), and ISO 27001 talks about providing measures to continuously improve an organization's Information Security Management Systems (ISMS). Finally, data allows organizations to measure the effectiveness of a given strategy: When strategies are put into place to overcome a challenge, collecting data will allow you to determine how well your solution is performing, and whether or not your approach needs to be tweaked or changed over the long term.

5

Fortifying the Fortress

Strategies for Robust Data Protection

5.1 Encryption Techniques

Encryption works by encoding "plaintext" into "ciphertext," typically through the use of cryptographic mathematical models known as algorithms. To decode the data back to plaintext requires the use of a decryption key, a string of numbers or a password also created by an algorithm. Most internet security (IS) professionals break down encryption into three distinct methods: symmetric, asymmetric and hashing.

There are two types of encryptions in widespread use today: symmetric and asymmetric encryption. The name derives from whether or not the same key is used for encryption and decryption. Encryption in cybersecurity is the conversion of data from a readable format into an encoded format. Encrypted data can only be read or processed after it's been decrypted. Encryption is the basic building block of data security. Data encryption converts data from a readable, plaintext format into an unreadable, encoded format such as ciphertext. Users and processes can only read and process encrypted data after it is decrypted. The decryption key is secret, so it must be protected against unauthorized access. Column-level encryption allows each column within a database table to have a unique decryption key. Symmetric encryption uses one private key to decrypt data retrieved from the database. Asymmetric encryption requires each authorized user to have a separate, unique and private key in order to decrypt data. Network encryption cracking is the breaching of network encryptions such as WEP and WPA, usually done through the use of special encryption cracking software. It may be done through a range of attacks such as active and passive, including injecting traffic, decrypting traffic and dictionary-based attacks. Data needs to be encrypted when it is in two different states at rest, when it is stored, such as in a database or in transit, and while it is being accessed or transmitted between parties. An encryption algorithm is a mathematical formula used to transform plaintext data into ciphertext. Decryption is the process of transforming unreadable data into readable format. Encryption is used to protect data from unauthorized

DOI: 10.1201/9781003604679-5

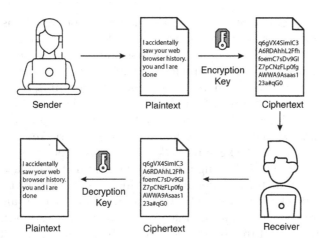

FIGURE 5.1
The encryption techniques.

access, while decryption is used to restore data to its original format. It helps protect private information, sensitive data, and can enhance the security of communication between client apps and servers. In essence, when data is encrypted, even if an unauthorized person or entity gains access to it, they will not be able to read it (Figure 5.1).

Encryption is among the most critical and widespread data security tools. By encoding plain text as ciphertext, encryption helps organizations protect data against a range of cyberattacks, including ransomware and other malware. Encryption is used to protect data from being stolen, changed or compromised and works by scrambling data into a secret code that can only be unlocked with a unique digital key. AI systems can be hacked or manipulated, leading to various cybersecurity implications. Attacks on AI systems include data poisoning, adversarial attacks, model inversion and evasion attacks. In traditional cryptography, AI is mainly used for cryptanalysis.

By training machine learning algorithms to recognize patterns and deviations in encrypted data, they can anticipate potential encryption keys and decode encrypted texts without the key. Typically, RSA keys are 2048 or 3072 bits long. While RSA is fundamental to many cryptographic protocols and applications, it is significantly slower than AES due to its complex mathematical operations. The emergence of quantum computers and AI pose a serious threat to traditional encryption methods. AI systems can be vulnerable to adversarial attacks, where malicious actors intentionally manipulate or deceive the system by introducing subtle changes to input data. Moreover, blockchain utilizes public key cryptography for the security of transactions. Each user on a blockchain network has a public-private key pair. Users sign transactions with their private keys, while others on the network use the corresponding public keys to verify the signature. Bitcoin, as well as Ethereum and many other cryptocurrencies, use a technology called public-private key encryption. This allows them to be trustless and makes secure transactions between strangers possible without a trusted intermediary like a bank or PayPal in the middle. By utilizing cryptographic algorithms, blockchain systems can guarantee the confidentiality of classified information and maintain transaction integrity. Three main types of cryptography are employed in blockchain: symmetric-key cryptography, asymmetric-key cryptography and hash functions. Blockchains make use of two types of cryptographic algorithms: asymmetric-key algorithms and hash functions. Hash functions are used to provide the functionality of a single view of blockchain to every participant. Blockchains generally use the SHA-256 hashing algorithm as their hash function. For example, Bitcoin uses Secure Hash Algorithm 256-bit (SHA-256) to encrypt the information from a block, ensuring data integrity by converting information into a hash, which is a unique 64-digit hexadecimal number in the blockchain.

Cryptography is the mathematical and computational practice of encoding and decoding data. Cryptocurrency generally uses two different cryptographic methods, one dedicated to generating its public-private key pairs and another for the purpose of validating transactions. Blockchain security methods include the use of public-key cryptography. A public key is a long, random-looking string of numbers. That is an address on the blockchain. Value tokens sent across the network are recorded as belonging to that address. Cryptographic hashing is a process that involves coding the data or information on the blockchain into an unreadable, unchangeable and unhackable text. This method of encryption does not make use of keys but instead uses a cipher to form a hash value of a fixed length from the plaintext. Bitcoin uses the SHA-256 hashing algorithm to encrypt hash the data stored in the blocks on the blockchain. Simply put, transaction data stored in a block is encrypted into a 256-bit (64-digit) hexadecimal number. That number contains all the transaction data and information linked to the blocks before that block. Symmetric encryption is generally faster than asymmetric encryption, as it requires less computational power, making it suitable for encrypting large amounts of data. In symmetric encryption, secure key distribution is crucial, as the same key is used for both encryption and decryption. Symmetric encryption is faster and simpler, but is often viewed as less secure than asymmetric encryption.

The Advanced Encryption Standard is a symmetric encryption algorithm that is the most frequently used method of data encryption globally. Often referred to as the gold standard for data encryption, AES is used by many government bodies worldwide, including in the U.S. AES 256-bit encryption is the strongest and most robust encryption standard that is commercially available today. While it is theoretically true that AES

256-bit encryption is harder to crack than AES 128-bit encryption, AES 128-bit encryption has never been cracked. To encrypt a message with the Caesar cipher, each letter of message is replaced by the letter three positions later in the alphabet. Hence, A is replaced by D, B by E, C by F, etc. Finally, X, Y and Z are replaced by A, B and C, respectively. So, for example, "WIKIPEDIA" encrypts as "ZLNLSHGLD." Triple Data Encryption Standard (DES) is a symmetric encryption technique and a more advanced form of the Data Encryption Standard (DES) method that encrypts data blocks using a 56-bit key. Triple DES applies the DES cipher algorithm three times to each data block.

WhatsApp provides end-to-end encryption for all personal messages that you send and receive. This makes sure that only you and the person you're talking to can read or listen to them. With end-to-end encrypted backup, you can add that same layer of protection to your iCloud and Google Account backups. It helps protect private information and sensitive data, and it can enhance the security of communication between client apps and servers. In essence, when data is encrypted, even if an unauthorized person or entity gains access to it, they will not be able to read it. AES stands out as one of the fastest encryption methods, especially for large data sets. Symmetric encryption methods like AES, Blowfish and Twofish are typically faster than asymmetric methods for vast amounts of data. The easiest encryption method is Asymmetric Encryption, as it uses only one key.

The main components of an encryption system are: (1) plaintext (not encrypted message), (2) encryption algorithm (works like a locking mechanism to a safe), (3) key (works like the safe's combination) and (4) ciphertext (produced from plaintext message by encryption key). Transport Layer Security Inspection (TLSI), also known as Transport Layer Security (TLS) break and inspect, is a security mechanism that allows enterprises to decrypt traffic, inspect the decrypted content for threats and then re-encrypt the traffic before it enters or leaves the network (Figure 5.2).

Modern encryption schemes use the concepts of public-key and symmetric-key. Modern techniques ensure security because modern computers are inefficient at cracking the encryption. Since 2010, HTTPS has been the default when you're signed into Gmail. This means that while your email travels between Google's data centers and the computer you use to read your email, it's encrypted and secure. Certain browsers support end-to-end encrypted chats on Messenger and Facebook. This means that the browser you are using determines whether can see all end-to-end encrypted chats, or whether those chats are hidden. As a result, encryption scrambles passwords so they're unreadable or unusable by hackers. That simple step protects your password while it's sitting in a server, and it offers more protection as your password zooms across the internet.

Symmetric Encryption

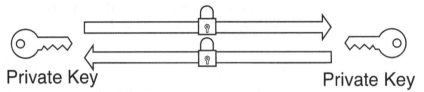

Private Key   Private Key

Asymmetric Encryption

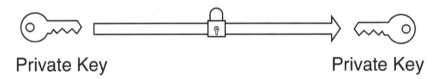

Private Key   Private Key

FIGURE 5.2
Symmetric and asymmetric encryption.

5.2 Access Controls and Authentication Methods

Authentication is any process by which a system verifies the identity of a user who wishes to access the system. In authentication, the user or computer has to prove its identity to the server or client. Usually, authentication by a server entails the use of a username and password. Other ways to authenticate can be through cards, retina scans, voice recognition and fingerprints. Now the property of being genuine and being able to be verified and trusted, confidence in the validity of a transmission, message, or message originator. The most accurate definition of authentication in cybersecurity is the process of verifying the identity of a user or device before granting access to a system or resources. Biometric authentication uses AI and deep learning techniques to confirm a user's identity using biometric information, or physical characteristics. This can include fingerprint, iris, palm or face recognition that uses deep learning, classification algorithms or neural networks to verify biometric information. Artificial intelligence and 2FA authentication combine to create powerful security tools. AI-based user authorization methods, such as facial recognition, voice authentication and behavior analysis, complement traditional 2FA authorization methods, making systems more reliable and secure. AI verification mechanisms are tools that ensure regulatory compliance by discouraging or detecting the illicit use of AI by a system or illicit AI control over a system. AI-based biometric authentication is identification based on their special and peculiar physical, behavioral or biological characteristics. AI validation performs a comprehensive assessment of security and safety vulnerabilities so you can understand the risks and protect yourself against them.

A new study shows an AI-based system has learned to correlate a person's unique fingerprints with a high degree of accuracy. According to the researchers, it does this by analyzing the curvature of the swirls at the center of the fingerprint rather than the minutiae, or endpoints in fingerprint ridges. There are four types of authentication based on using something you know: password, PIN, Personally Identifiable Information (PII) or an answer to a security question. Some methods have objects, such as key cards or ID badges. Some are based on what you are: facial or iris recognition, fingerprints or biometric data.

The role of AI in AI-powered authentication involves the use of machine learning algorithms to analyze user behavior, detect anomalies and verify identities in real time. It can adapt to dynamic patterns and learn from user interactions. This means that AI provides continuous authentication. Moreover, blockchain utilizes public key cryptography for the security of transactions. Each user on a blockchain network has a public-private key pair. Users sign transactions with their private keys, while others on the network use the corresponding public keys to verify the signature. This process seeks to prevent unauthorized users from gaining access to an account with nothing more than a stolen password. The two factors involved in the 2FA process include a knowledge factor, such as a password or PIN, and a possession factor, which could be a smart card, security token or mobile device.

Because access control is typically based on the identity of the user who requests access to a resource, authentication is essential to effective security. The four types of access control are:

- Discretionary access control (DAC)
- Mandatory access control (MAC)
- Role-based access control (RBAC)
- Rule-based access control (RuBAC)

The most common authentication methods are Password Authentication Protocol (PAP), Authentication Token, Symmetric-Key Authentication and Biometric Authentication. Secure access control uses policies that verify users are who they claim to be and ensures appropriate control access levels are granted to users. While mandatory access control systems are the most secure type of access control, they're also the most inflexible as they only allow the system's owner or administrator to control and manage access. People are given access based on different security levels and information clearance. Since access control models include Mandatory Access Control (MAC), Role Based Access Control (RBAC), Discretionary Access Control (DAC) and Rule-Based Access Control (RBAC), which define the level of permissions. Taken together, this process ensures that only trusted users have access to important resources. On Cisco routers, there are two main types: standard and extended. These are the most widely used ACLs, but there are

**Multi-Factor
Authentication**

FIGURE 5.3
Access controls and authentication methods.

some advanced ACLs as well. Some of the advanced ACLs include reflexive ACLs and dynamic ACLs. While authentication is the process of identifying users that request access to a system, network or device, access control often determines user identity according to credentials like username and password (Figure 5.3).

Typically, users prove they are who they say they are by entering a password, something only the user is supposed to know, but to strengthen security, many organizations also require that they prove their identity with something they have such as a phone or token device.

Access control is an essential element of security that determines who is allowed to access certain data, apps and resources—and in what circumstances. In the same way that keys and preapproved guest lists protect physical spaces, access control policies protect digital spaces. Consequently, security is the main reason why access control is important. Its aim is to protect a building and its occupants, data and assets by reducing the risk of unauthorized intrusion, while making access convenient for authorized users and approved visitors. These techniques can provide other important benefits, too. Furthermore, authentication methods include something users know, something users have and something users are. Not every authentication type is created equal to protect the network, however; these authentication methods range from offering basic protection to stronger security. Biometric authentication relies on the unique biological traits of a user in order to verify their identity. This makes biometrics one of the most secure authentication methods as of today. Likewise, there are three basic types of authentication. Knowledge-based is something like a password or PIN code that only the identified user would know. Property-based means the user possesses an access card, key, key fob or authorized device unique to them. The simplest authentication method is HTTP basic authentication (BA) implementation, which does not require cookies, session identifiers or login pages; rather, HTTP Basic authentication uses standard fields in the HTTP header. Multi-factor authentication is a quick and simple way to add an extra layer of protection to confidential data. This additional step acts like an extra lock designed to protect accounts from hackers or a cybersecurity weakness. In some cases, MFA might require biometric verification, like a fingerprint or facial scan.

5.3 Data Anonymization and Pseudonymization

Pseudonymization is the process of replacing identifying information with random codes, which can be linked back to the original person with extra information, whereas anonymization is the irreversible process of rendering personal data non-personal, and not subject to the GDPR. An example of data pseudonymization is where the "Age" data could be encrypted with an X key and the "Last name" and "First name" values with a Y key.

Data anonymization is a method of information sanitization which involves removing or encrypting personally identifiable data in a dataset. The goal is to ensure the privacy of the subject's information. Data anonymization minimizes the risk of information leaks when data is moving across boundaries. For example, anonymized data is a dataset that has been stripped of any personally identifiable information such as names, addresses and phone numbers. This type of data can be used to analyze trends and patterns without the risk of exposing any individual's personal information. In the context of blockchain, anonymity can be achieved by using pseudonymous addresses, which are unique strings of characters representing a user's identity on the blockchain. These addresses are generated through a cryptographic process and are not directly linked to a person's real-world identity. Data is stored in blocks that are immutable; new data can be added to the blockchain, but once the data has been added, it cannot be changed or removed anymore. The distribution and immutability aspects of blockchain technology lead to challenges in becoming compliant with the right to erasure of the GDPR. Monero (XMR) is the undisputed king of privacy-focused cryptocurrencies. Launched in 2014, it has established itself as the most private, secure and untraceable digital currency available. Monero's advanced privacy features make it virtually impossible to trace transactions or connect them to individual users. Blockchain technology never requires an organization to reveal more data than it is comfortable with. On-chain data can also be encrypted so that it is only usable by permissioned parties. Although transactions are recorded publicly in the blockchain network, pseudonymity offers a layer of privacy. It's like using a pen name, wherein you operate under a false identity, such as a blockchain address, that doesn't directly reveal your real name. Pseudonymity means using a pseudonym instead of one's real name. Examples include pen names of authors such as Mark Twain or Cecil Adams, as well as stage names of performers such as Woody Allen or Ice T. Usernames used online, if not connected to a person's legal identity, are examples of pseudonyms.

Data masking is usually irreversible, meaning that you cannot recover the original data from the masked data. The difference between anonymous and anonymized information is—Anonymous data: Data that never had identifiable markers to begin with.

Anonymized data: Data that once contained identifiable markers but has since been processed to remove or alter them for privacy reasons.

There are a variety of methods available to anonymize data, such as directory replacement (modifying the individual's name while maintaining consistency between values), scrambling (obfuscation; the process can sometimes be reversible) and masking (hiding a part of the data with random characters). Pseudonymization of data means replacing any information which could be used to identify an individual with a pseudonym, or, in other words, a value which does not allow the individual to be directly identified. Pseudonym means "false name" in Greek, and a famous example is the fictional character Bruce Wayne, who sometimes goes by the name Batman. Similar to Bruce Wayne and Batman, pseudonymization in IT systems means that you mask the registered user and their personal data. Although it's not sufficient on its own, pseudonymization can support an enterprise's efforts to comply with data protection laws by reducing the risk of unauthorized access to sensitive data. In the event of a data breach, pseudonymization makes it more difficult for attackers to identify and access sensitive data.

Other examples include anonymizing information on credit card numbers by replacing all but the last four digits by "X," or NRIC numbers, which may be represented by "S0XXXX45A" instead of the full set of original digits Anonymous information is not personal data, and data protection law does not apply. However, there are five types of data anonymization operations: generalization, suppression, anatomization, permutation and perturbation. Meanwhile, truly anonymized data, whether in an aggregated form or not, can be freely used and shared; the ability to glean personal information from both anonymized and aggregated data creates risks for using and disclosing such data for commercial purposes because there is always a risk of re-identification. However, pseudonymization provides moderate data protection. Since pseudonymization is reversible, it may only partially prevent the possibility of re-identification. However, it significantly reduces linkage to original identities. Tokenization is like pseudonymization on steroids, encrypting your PII and replacing your pseudonym with an unrecognizable token. As a result, anonymity means that an individual dealing with an APP entity cannot be identified and the entity does not collect personal information or identifiers. A pseudonym is a name, term or descriptor that is different from an individual's actual name.

5.4 Backup and Disaster Recovery Plans

This plan outlines steps to take to restore critical systems and data, minimize downtime and get the business back up and running as quickly as possible. By having a DRP for cybersecurity in place, organizations can lessen the impact of a security incident, protect sensitive data and ensure business continuity. Backup and recovery is the process of duplicating data and storing it in a secure place in case of loss or damage, and then restoring that data to a location the original one or a safe alternative so it can be used again in operations. It's a set of written instructions enabling a timely response to data breaches, insider threats and other cybersecurity incidents. An IRP elaborates measures to detect and identify an incident, respond to it, mitigate its consequences and ensure it won't reoccur. Disaster recovery testing is a fundamental component of an organization's business continuity and disaster recovery plan. It involves simulating a disaster, like a cyberattack with ransomware, a data breach, power outage or natural disaster, to assess an organization's ability to regain control over its IT systems. Cyber-recovery specifically refers to a responsive solution involving the processes and measures put in place to restore and recover data, systems and services after a cyber-incident. The plan should include a strategy to ensure that all critical information is backed up. Identify critical software applications and data and the hardware required to run them. Using standardized hardware will help to replicate and reimage new hardware. Backup and recovery is the process of creating a copy of our critical data, storing it in a secure place and then restoring that data to its original location or a safe alternative in case of unexpected scenarios like hardware failure, accidental deletion, data corruption, cyberattacks and natural disasters. AI optimizes resource allocation during a disaster. It can reroute network traffic, allocate bandwidth to critical applications and prioritize recovery efforts. This resource optimization ensures that essential functions are restored quickly, while less critical operations can be addressed later. The integration of AI in disaster management offers several advantages that enhance the overall response capability such as early warning signs. AI-based algorithms can spot subtle signs of impending crises that might be missed by human analysts, thus providing decision-makers with vital advanced notice. AI-powered systems can be trained with the help of seismic data to analyze the magnitude and patterns of earthquakes and predict the location of earthquakes and aftershocks. Deep learning systems are being used to analyze massive volumes of seismic data collected by researchers. Generative AI changes the game by creating highly customized, dynamic recovery plans that take into account the specific nature of the disaster, the current state of the IT infrastructure and the criticality of different systems and data. After all, AI plays a pivotal role in reducing response times during emergencies. By analyzing real-time data, AI systems can predict potential disasters and automate dispatching processes. This ensures that emergency personnel are deployed swiftly to critical locations, potentially saving numerous lives. Furthermore, disaster response robots are robotic systems used for preventing outspread of disaster damage under emergent situations, such as for search and rescue, recovery construction, etc. Disaster changes its state as time passes. Through generative AI, computers can predict the most relevant patterns to input, allowing them to output corresponding content. During the training, a limited number of parameters are given to the generative AI models, enabling them to make their own conclusions and highlight features present in the training data. AI is used to enhance disaster response by predicting natural weather disasters and helping first responders make better decisions about resource allocation and evacuation routes. AI can also analyze data from disasters to create predictive models and identify vulnerabilities. It can detect unknown or emerging threats by identifying deviations from standard baselines of what is considered normal. Advanced AI algorithms, such as deep learning and neural networks, can analyze vast data sets for suspicious patterns, using existing intelligence to improve their predictive capabilities over time. Researchers have been able to predict tsunami amplitudes by combining data from the Global Navigation Satellite System with artificial intelligence. Early warnings of earthquakes may also be possible using AI technology. AI and machine learning can be used for hurricane forecasting as well.

Blockchain integration with backup creates a certificate for each file. This certificate connects the file with its permanent record in the chain, allowing enterprises to check and validate the file's authenticity. The data stored in a blockchain is decentralized, meaning that it is not stored in a single location or controlled by a single entity. Instead, the data is stored on multiple devices, or nodes, which are connected to the blockchain network. If access to a private key is lost, you cannot recover it from the public address. The best option is to use a backup of your wallet or recovery seed phrase if available to restore access. Always keep private key and recovery information secure to prevent loss of funds. Private keys can also be used to restore access to Bitcoin; download a wallet app that allows importing private keys. Open the app and select Import to find the option to import or restore a wallet. Now block-level backup explained the legacy backup format.

Block-level backup uploads only modified file parts, as opposed to incremental or full backups that upload whole files. Block-level backup occupies less bandwidth and reduces backup duration. When you download or update the blockchain.com app that is available from version 2.57.0 on iOS and version 6.36.3 on Android and sign up or log in, your wallet is automatically backed up to Apple iCloud or your Google Drive account. If you haven't made a wallet recovery phrase yet, you will be prompted to do so during your first blockchain.com account withdrawal. Never share your recovery phrase with third parties as it may lead to a loss of funds. By sending requests to the blockchain's API endpoints, developers can fetch specific information such as transaction details or smart contract events. Full Node Operation is running a full node; it involves maintaining a complete copy of the blockchain's data on your own hardware. When you get back to the previous tab and click the Forgot your password? button, enter the email address that you used to create the account and click Request password reset button. Then you will receive an email for an password reset link.

A backup and disaster recovery plan is a set of policies and software solutions that work together to maintain business continuity in the event of a security incident. These plans typically include guidance on how to properly restore data with the backup software used by the organization. Although the sub-processes—'backup' and 'disaster recovery'—are sometimes mistaken for each other or for the entire process, backup is the process of making the file copies, and disaster recovery is the plan and processes for using the copies to quickly reestablish access to applications, data and IT resources after an outage.

A good ISO 27001 disaster recovery plan ensures that business operations can be restored in the event of a disruption, allowing you to minimize downtime and continue functioning without interruption. Typically, disaster recovery involves securely replicating and backing up critical data and workloads to a secondary location or multiple locations—disaster recovery sites. A disaster recovery site can be used to recover data from the most recent backup or a previous point in time. There are seven main components of any good disaster recovery plan. These include mapping out your assets, identifying your assets' criticality and context, conducting a risk assessment, defining your recovery objectives, choosing a disaster recovery setup, budgeting for your setup and testing and reviewing the plan. Since a disaster recovery plan describes scenarios for resuming work quickly and reducing interruptions in the aftermath of a disaster, it is an important part of the business continuity plan and it allows for sufficient IT recovery and the prevention of data loss. The services offered by data centers (DC) should be available, either in full or in limited form, from Disaster Recovery (DR) in case of the former's failure. For example, the system should allow live monitoring of a subset of cameras even when the data center (DC) is unserviceable. The plan should define who in the organization is responsible for disaster recovery processes, with their names and contact details. Critical responsibilities include:

- Ongoing backups and maintenance of business continuity systems.
- Responsibility for declaring a disaster.

Disaster recovery is an organization's method of regaining access and functionality to its IT infrastructure after events like a natural disaster, cyberattack or even business disruptions related to the COVID-19 pandemic. A variety of disaster recovery methods can be part of a disaster recovery plan. Inventorying all assets—hardware, software, data and network resources—is a critical starting point for an effective disaster recovery plan. Rank the assets based on their importance to business functions. The most common issue, occurring in 62% of all recovery plans, are errors in the plan itself. This is often due to the plan not being kept up to date (47%) and the unavailability of or inaccurate passwords (34%). A Another reason for failure is insufficient backup power—22%. Furthermore, disaster recovery testing verifies the effectiveness of your disaster recovery plan to ensure your organization can restore data and applications to continue operations after a disruption, such as a natural disaster, IT failure or cyberattack. Hence, the purpose of a DR environment is to have a production mirror deployed in a different geolocation/data center to ensure production uptime should the actual production server go down. The term "cloud disaster recovery" (cloud DR) refers to the strategies and services that enterprises apply for the purpose of backing up applications, resources and data into a cloud environment. Cloud DR helps protect corporate resources and ensure business continuity. Likewise, the Disaster Recovery Plan should be prepared by the Disaster Recovery Committee, which should include representatives from all critical departments or areas of the department's functions. As a result, the disaster management cycle is a framework that defines the stages of a disaster. It can be used by both organizations and individuals to prepare for and respond to disasters of every kind, including natural disasters, technological disasters and human-made disasters.

5.5 Security Best Practices

Using strong passwords, updating your software, thinking before you click on suspicious links and turning on multi-factor authentication are the basics of what we call "cyber hygiene" and will drastically improve your online safety. These cybersecurity basics apply to both individuals and organizations. Though the five C's of cybersecurity —Change, Continuity, Cost,

Compliance and Coverage—highlighting their importance in modern-day digital defense mechanisms. The digital landscape is an ever-evolving realm where securing assets against threats has become paramount.

A best practice is a safety- or security-related practice, technique, process or program attribute observed during an appraisal that may merit consideration by other DOE and contractor organizations for implementation because it has been demonstrated to substantially improve safety or security performance. Security best practices for companies are:

- Communicate with insurance company.
- Consider engaging an MSSP.
- Educate employees.
- Perform shadow IT assessments regularly.
- Establish best practices for vendor management.
- Take website protection measures.
- Implement robust data encryption measures.

These are related to economic security, food security, health security, environmental security, personal security, community security and political security. Some of the criteria associated with economic security include insured basic income and employment and access to social safety nets. Fundamental principles of information security are confidentiality, integrity, availability and non-repudiation. The six Ps of security are: preparation, prevention, protection, professionalism, partnership and proficiency. By understanding these six Ps, businesses can choose the best private security company to keep their assets, employees and customers safe. Furthermore, there are examples of best practices:

- Maintaining constant communication with all stakeholders.
- Creating a risk response team.
- Developing a project brief.
- Creating a detailed project plan.
- Ensuring that document every step of the project completion process.

The three principles of security are confidentiality, integrity and availability. Every element of the information security program must be designed to implement one or more of these principles. Together, they are called the CIA Triad.

Furthermore, security measures, such as surveillance systems, access control and trained security personnel, provide a sense of safety and personal protection. They act as a deterrent against criminal activities, making individuals feel more secure in public spaces, workplaces, and residential areas.

Availability

FIGURE 5.4
The CIA triad.

Authentication is the most basic security activity. It is merely the process of determining if the credentials given by a user or another system (such as a username and password) are authorized to access the network resource in question (Figure 5.4). The security infrastructure includes security systems, access control, authentication systems and surveillance equipment that provide a comprehensive security solution for businesses. Meanwhile, security means safety, as well as the measures taken to be safe or protected. In order to provide adequate security for the parade, town officials often hire extra guards. A small child will sometimes latch onto a blanket or stuffed animal that gives him or her the feeling of security. A security classification (PROTECTED, SECRET and TOP SECRET) is only applied to information (or assets that hold information, such as laptops or USBs) if it requires protection, because the impact of compromise of the information or asset would be high, extreme or catastrophic. Best practices are a set of guidelines, ethics or ideas that represent the most efficient or prudent course of action in a given business situation. Though "Best Practices" are the best-known method, technique or proven processes used to achieve an end goal—a "standard." Standards are usually established by an authority (a rule or principle) or by general consent (de facto standards) as a basis of comparison. A best practice is a method or technique that has been generally accepted as superior to other known alternatives because it often produces results that are superior to those achieved by other means or because it has become a standard way of doing things. Consequently, knowledge security is first and foremost about preventing the undesirable transfer of sensitive knowledge and technology. Transfer is undesirable if it compromises our country's national security. Knowledge security also entails the covert influencing of education and research by other states. As a result, malware has become one of the most significant external threats to systems. Malware can cause widespread damage and disruption, and preventing it requires huge efforts within most organizations. The CIA triad does not consider the criticality of information to be protected. It doesn't address the need to prioritize information based on its relationship to processes that are critical to meeting business goals. Today, the CIA triad remains foundational and useful. However, an alternative to the CIA triad is the Parkerian hexad. That is an advanced version of the CIA triad with a set of six elements of information security: confidentiality, possession, integrity, authenticity, availability and utility. Furthermore, by using the CIA triad, organizations mitigate unauthorized access to keep data secret, they backup and maintain the integrity of the data against ransomware attacks and they keep data available. If the data is not available to the right parties, it's the same as if the data doesn't exist. The opposite of confidentiality, integrity and availability is disclosure, alteration and destruction. The CIA triad is important because it helps organizations prioritize their security efforts, identify vulnerabilities and respond to cyberattacks more effectively. It also serves as a framework for incident response, allowing organizations to evaluate what went wrong and how to prevent future attacks.

6

Building a Culture of Security

Training, Development, and Response

6.1 Employee Training and Awareness Programs

Training and awareness is a support process that ensures staff members have the knowledge and skills to perform their work, including work in other processes such as incident management, controls management and risk management. Training and awareness typically take place at various levels of an organization. A staff awareness programmer:

1 Helps companies identify potential security problems.
2 Helps staff understand the consequences of poor information security and cyber-security.
3 Ensures procedures are followed consistently.

Training and awareness are important because training helps stop unauthorized access. While phishing emails are commonly used by cybercriminals to gain unauthorized access to company systems, security awareness training also helps businesses prevent other forms of unauthorized access, such as physical infiltration of premises.

The CISA Cybersecurity Awareness Program is a national public awareness effort aimed at increasing the understanding of cyber threats and empowering the American public to be safer and more secure online. Cybersecurity is a shared responsibility and we each have a part to play. Security awareness training can help organizations reduce the risk of data breaches, malware infections, phishing attempts and other malicious activities. By providing employees with the knowledge and skills they need to stay safe online, organizations can ensure their data is secure and protected from cyberattacks. Cybersecurity awareness is an ongoing process of educating and training employees about the threats that lurk in cyberspace, how to prevent such threats, and what they must do in the event of a security incident. To raise awareness about cybersecurity, provide

DOI: 10.1201/9781003604679-6

regular training sessions, share frequent updates about new cyberattack techniques, conduct security assessments and use visual aids like posters and infographics to convey the dangers of cyber threats. Cyber awareness training educates employees about the wide variety of threats they may encounter or actions they may take that could jeopardize their organization's security. The primary objective of cybersecurity awareness training for employees is to equip and familiarize them with the knowledge to defend against cyber threats. Employees who are aware of how to defend against cyberattacks are better able to make smart security decisions and protect themselves as well as the organization. Cybercrime, also known as computer crime, involves a wide range of criminal activities that are carried out by using or targeting a computer or related system, especially illegally to access, transmit or manipulate data. User awareness is knowledge that leads to appropriate security behaviors. However, knowledge itself is insufficient. Awareness requires that people behave in accordance with that knowledge. For example, just because people know that they should not write down their password does not mean that they will not. IoT devices in manufacturing plants collect real-time data on machine performance, production rates and product quality. Situationally aware systems can detect anomalies or equipment failures, triggering maintenance alerts or adjusting production parameters to minimize downtime and maximize output. After all, this goes a step beyond theory of mind AI and understanding emotions to being aware of themselves, their state of being, and being able to sense or predict others' feelings.

Python is one of the most popular blockchain programming languages available. It's the best programming language to learn for blockchain; when compared to other programming languages, the syntax allows developers to write programs with fewer lines. The SDG Big Data Platform aims to integrate Big Earth Data for Sustainable Development Goals (SDGs) for monitoring and prediction and to provide decision support for implementing SDGs. Through the management of greenhouse gas emissions, companies are able to identify potential sources of emissions and find solutions to reduce them. Better management of resources and information relating to resource usage help minimize wastage of water, electricity or raw materials. The big data used for sustainable development seeks to collect, cross and relate data from physical components such as fires, droughts, rains, earthquakes etc. with data on social components such as light intensity per household, telephone calls, social networks activity and use of transport.

The primary purpose of awareness-based training is to sensitize employees on the importance of diversity in the workplace. It makes them aware of common assumptions and prejudices about other employees who are different from them. Consequently, training programs prepare employees with the necessary skills and knowledge they need to perform their daily tasks. Moreover, training programs provide employees with extensive knowledge in their respective fields, allowing them to become more experienced and comfortable doing their job. These levels are achieved by:

- Trainings and awareness programs.
- Regular face-to-face meetings and discussions.
- Regular newsletters or other communications.
- Learning corporate documents.
- Self-education.

Furthermore, the awareness sessions should include the signs of SE attack and role-playing of common situations. Without this awareness, many staff will offer up the information asked for by the intruder and the business totally misses the fact it has just been compromised. Risk awareness training in the workplace is about knowing what risks would be faced based on the location and the workplace, understanding how likely these risks are to occur and anticipating what should be done to prevent or mitigate harm. Meanwhile, awareness is important because being aware will give an insight into beliefs and whether they are positive or holding back. If we are aware, then this will give us knowledge, and if we have knowledge, then we know what we need to do to and the direction we need to go to make changes to improve and be successful. The purpose of ISO awareness training is to ensure that employees understand the principles, requirements and objectives of ISO standards, enabling them to contribute to compliance and continuous improvement efforts within the organization.

Effective training is considered to be a key factor for improved performance, as it can enhance the level of employee and firm competency. It provides support to fill the gap between desired performance and actual employee performance. The three principles of training that should be followed in developing fitness program are overload, progression and specificity. When you increase the repetitions, amount of weight, or length of time in an exercise you are accustomed to, that applies overload. The best ways to create awareness are:

- Set goals and identify KPIs.
- Select the right date for awareness campaigns.
- Identify and define audience.
- Invest in the right tools.
- Craft awareness campaign message.
- Engage ambassadors in peer-to-peer fundraising.
- Secure awareness campaign sponsors.

FIGURE 6.1
Awareness training.

Awareness is important in a team or group setting, and external self-awareness is crucial for collaboration. It helps team members understand each other's strengths, weaknesses and communication styles, facilitating better teamwork (Figure 6.1). Finally, awareness is the quality or state of being aware, and knowledge and understanding that something is happening or exists, promoting a heightened awareness of the problem.

6.2 Secure Software Development Practices

These are a set of processes and activities that organizations follow to ensure that their software is developed with security in mind. The goal of the SSDLC is to identify and mitigate potential security vulnerabilities and threats in the software development process, so that the final product is as secure as possible. To ensure security in software development:

- Embrace a security-first mindset.
- Utilize security tools.
- Regularly conduct security testing.
- Code review and audits.
- Stay updated and patch regularly.
- Secure development environment.
- Educate and train your team.
- Follow security frameworks and standards.

Secure software development is a methodology (often associated with DevSecOps) for creating software that incorporates security into every phase of the software development life cycle (SDLC). Security is baked into the code from inception, rather than being addressed after testing reveals critical product flaws. Integrate security measures throughout the software development life cycle (SDLC), ensuring continuous monitoring and vulnerability assessment. Additionally, employ a secure software framework, conduct regular security awareness training for your team and maintain up-to-date software and systems. Digital security controls include such things as usernames and passwords, two-factor authentication, antivirus software and firewalls. Cybersecurity controls include anything specifically designed to prevent attacks on data, including DDoS mitigation and intrusion prevention systems. Software security solutions help ensure data is protected while in transit and at rest. They also help protect against system vulnerabilities like malware and ransomware attacks. Preventing cyberattacks such as application security helps build protection around applications to make it harder for attackers to access systems and exploit vulnerabilities, reducing the likelihood of a cyberattack. Application security is the process of developing, adding and testing security features within applications to prevent security vulnerabilities against threats such as unauthorized access and modification. Secure software development makes the security of applications a core component of your SDLC. This methodology integrates security testing and other activities into all phases and facets of the development process, from planning to release, for an approach that's proactive as opposed to reactive. However, security testing is an important aspect of software testing focused on identifying and addressing security vulnerabilities in a software application. It aims to ensure that the software is secure from malicious attacks, unauthorized access and data breaches. Furthermore, software testing is the process of evaluating and verifying that a software product or application does what it's supposed to do. The benefits of good testing include preventing bugs and improving performance. By identifying vulnerabilities and potential attack vectors, security testing enables organizations to fortify their defenses and maintain clients' trust and confidence. Some of the reasons security testing is crucial include being a proactive approach to mitigating cyber-risks.

QA security testing ensures software stays safe from hackers by checking for weaknesses. It involves testing security features to find loopholes that could be exploited. Techniques like penetration testing and code review are used to assess how resilient a software is. So that search for security testing is a combination of the testing techniques used to test the application for security problems. It is mainly used to test the security of the data and functionalities of the application. The security control assessment, formerly known as a Security Test and Evaluation (ST&E), is an evaluation of the controls protecting an information system.

Secure code review is a manual or automated process that examines an application's source code. The goal of this examination is to identify any existing security flaws or vulnerabilities. Code review specifically looks for logic errors, examines spec implementation and checks style guidelines, among other activities. A secure code review specifically looks for security-related issues, such as input validation problems, authentication and authorization flaws, data leakage, hardcoded data, SQL injection, Cross-Site Scripting (XSS) and other vulnerabilities that could be exploited by attackers. A software code audit is a comprehensive analysis of source code in a programming project with the intent of discovering bugs, security breaches or violations of programming conventions. It is an integral part of the defensive programming paradigm, which attempts to reduce errors before the software is released. A security audit includes an evaluation of all networks and hardware involved with a company, while a security assessment only scans the company's technological systems and identifies flaws. Reviews are typically done by fellow developers during the development process. Code audits, on the other hand, can be done by internal teams or external experts and provide a more independent in-depth analysis. A secure code review is a technique for locating security bugs early in the software development lifecycle (SDLC). Reviewers audit an application's source code to verify that it has proper security and logical controls in place. The review is most effective when combined with automated and manual penetration testing. Secure coding is the practice of developing computer software in a way that guards against the accidental introduction of security vulnerabilities. Reviewers audit an application's source code to verify that it has proper security and logical controls in place. The review is most effective when combined with automated and manual penetration testing. A software audit is a thorough review of a software product to check its quality, progress, standards and regulations. It basically checks the health of a product and ensures that everything is going as planned. It can be done by an internal team or by external independent auditors.

Patches are software and operating system (OS) updates that address security vulnerabilities within a program or product. Software vendors may choose to release updates to fix performance bugs, as well as to provide enhanced security features. Furthermore, a more secure environment, when regularly patching vulnerabilities, helps to manage and reduce the risks that exist in the environment. This helps protect organizations from potential security breaches. However, a patch is a targeted fix for a specific issue or vulnerability, while an update is a more comprehensive upgrade that includes various improvements and changes. Beyond security, the impact of regular updates on system performance and resource optimization cannot be overstated. These updates ensure that software operates at peak efficiency, leveraging technological advancements to reduce system load, enhance speed and improve overall user satisfaction. Patching is required to keep a system's stability and safety. It breaks down software weaknesses, preventing cyber threats like viruses and hackers from entering the system. Regular updates eliminate errors, improve speed and increase software stability. Patch management is the process of applying updates to software, drivers and firmware to protect against vulnerabilities. Effective patch management also helps ensure the best operating performance of systems by boosting productivity. In general, patches are important software updates that repair any errors or bugs that were detected by the program. They address any potential vulnerabilities before they get worse by replacing older data with a newer version to support and cover any weaknesses that were exposed by a hacking or cybercrime attempt. With antivirus updates, the developers often continue to improve their products to keep them safe from new viruses and malware.

The secure coding practices in SDLC formalize and document the software development life cycle (SDLC) processes to incorporate major components of a development process. Hence, the best practices for secure SDLC are:

- Specify requirements.
- Perform security audits.
- Educate developers on best coding practices, tools and frameworks.
- Conduct an architectural risk analysis at the beginning.
- Tackle the big problems first.
- Secure planning and building for test cases.
- Use code-scanning tools.

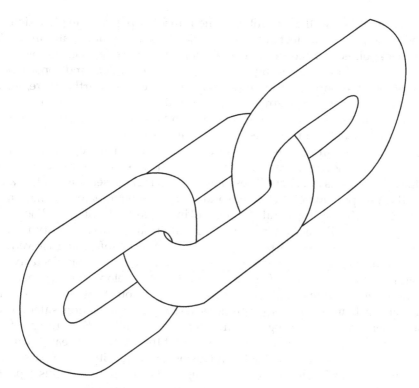

FIGURE 6.2
Software security.

Furthermore, there are a number of security software categories, but some of the more common ones include: antivirus, antispyware and firewall software (Figure 6.2). Antivirus software protects computer from viruses, while antispyware software protects computer from spyware and other malicious programs. Software security is critical because software vulnerabilities can lead to cyberattacks, data breaches and major disruptions of computer systems. As more critical systems rely on software, the impact of insecure software grows more severe. Consequently, the main secure design principles are the following: a) Economy of mechanism: Keep the design as simple and small as possible. b) Fail-safe defaults: Base access decisions on permission rather than exclusion. c) Complete mediation: Every access to every object must be checked for authority (there and then).

The goal of NIST's secure software development framework is to help reduce the number of vulnerabilities in software released to production environments, as well as to mitigate the impact of potential exploitation of unaddressed and undetected vulnerabilities. Security quality gates in SDLC are checkpoints that require deliverables to meet specific, measurable success criteria before progressing. They help foster confidence and consistency throughout the entire software development lifecycle. Furthermore, each company will have a designated team of individuals, usually including a Chief Information Security Officer (CISO) and an IT director, spearheading this initiative, but the reality is that all employees are responsible in some capacity for ensuring the security of their company's sensitive data. After all, the purpose of security features is to reduce the risk of damage to items of value by malicious attackers. These items could include sensitive data, valuable IP, safe operation of the system and even the reputation of the manufacturing brand. Safety is generally thought of in terms of data integrity. Backups, checksums, etc all ensure that the data is safe from failure. Security is protecting data from unauthorized access, such as private info being viewed by a trojan, or database tables being dropped from SQL injection. Security by design is an approach to software and hardware development that seeks to make systems as free of vulnerabilities and impervious to attack as possible through such measures as continuous testing, authentication safeguards and adherence to best programming practices. Finally, OS security refers to specified steps or measures used to protect the OS from threats, viruses, worms, malware or remote hacker intrusions. OS security encompasses all preventive-control techniques, which safeguard any computer assets capable of being stolen, edited or deleted if OS security is compromised.

6.3 Network Security Measures (Firewalls, Intrusion Detection Systems, etc.)

Network security protects network and data from breaches, intrusions and other threats. This is a vast and overarching term that describes hardware and software solutions as well as processes or rules and configurations relating to network use, accessibility and overall threat protection. This encompasses measures aimed at protecting people and assets from intrusions, burglaries, fires, accidents and other incidents. For instance, physical security systems include surveillance cameras, motion detectors, alarm systems, secure doors and windows and more. When there are four main types of security: debt securities, equity securities, derivative securities and hybrid securities, which are a combination of debt and equity.

Protective measures (safety)—all preventive measures to protect places, institutions or persons; for example, fire safety standards or conditions for flood-prone buildings. Security measures (security) —all preventive measures taken to secure places, institutions or persons, e.g. threat analyses.

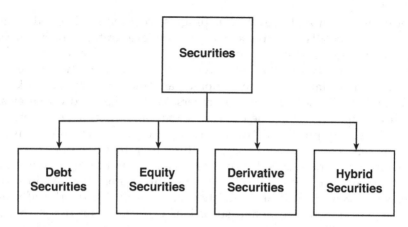

FIGURE 6.3
Various securities.

Network security is any activity designed to protect the usability and integrity of your network and data. It includes both hardware and software technologies (Figure 6.3). It targets a variety of threats. It stops them from entering or spreading on the network. Effective network security manages access to the network. The network security model is the structure and layers of defense used to protect network and data confidentiality, integrity and availability. Key components of a strong network security model include firewalls, intrusion detection systems, data encryption, endpoint security and network access controls, among others. Firewalls are network security systems that prevent unauthorized access to a network. It can be a hardware or software unit that filters the incoming and outgoing traffic within a private network, according to a set of rules to spot and prevent cyberattacks. Firewalls are used in enterprise and personal settings. After all, a firewall is a network security device that monitors incoming and outgoing network traffic and decides whether to allow or block specific traffic based on a defined set of security rules. Firewalls have been a first line of defense in network security for over 25 years. Firewall performance is measured by the throughput of HTTP traffic. This throughput refers to the amount of data that the firewall can process in a given time and is usually expressed in megabits per second (Mbps) or gigabits per second (Gbps). The measurements are based on a response size of 512 KB. Furthermore, a firewall is a security system designed to prevent unauthorized access into or out of a computer network. Firewalls are often used to make sure internet users without access are not able to interface with private networks, or intranets, connected to the internet. Firewalls provide protection against outside cyberattackers by shielding your computer or network from malicious or unnecessary network traffic. Firewalls can also prevent malicious software from accessing a computer or network via the internet. The three main types of firewalls (packet-filtering, stateful inspection and proxy) offer progressively more advanced protection levels. Firewalls don't inspect application-level traffic, which can lead to blocking safe traffic or websites such as YouTube under certain circumstances. A firewall can either be software or hardware. Software firewalls are programs installed on each computer, and they regulate network traffic through applications and port numbers. Meanwhile, hardware firewalls are the equipment established between the gateway and your network. Network security protects network and data from breaches, intrusions and other threats. This is a vast and overarching term that describes hardware and software solutions as well as processes or rules and configurations relating to network use, accessibility and overall threat protection. An intrusion detection system (IDS) is an application that monitors network traffic and searches for known threats and suspicious or malicious activity. The IDS sends alerts to IT and security teams when it detects any security risks and threats. Furthermore, network security measures are the tools and technologies such as firewalls and intrusion prevention systems (IPS) that are added to a network to secure stored or transmitted data, voice and video. Hence a network-based intrusion detection system (NIDS) detects malicious traffic on a network. NIDS usually require promiscuous network access in order to analyze all traffic, including all unicast traffic. NIDS are passive devices that do not interfere with the traffic they monitor (see Figure 6.4).

Network intrusion detection systems monitor inbound and outbound traffic to devices across the network. NIDS are placed at strategic points in the network, often immediately behind firewalls at the network perimeter, so

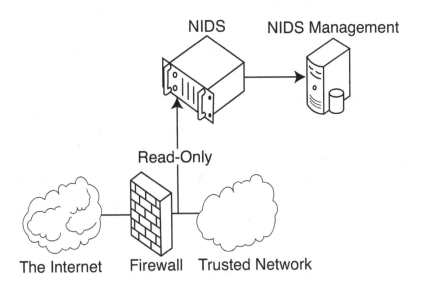

FIGURE 6.4
Network-based intrusion detection system (NIDS).

that they can flag any malicious traffic breaking through. Furthermore, there are three primary areas or classifications of security controls: management security, operational security and physical security controls.

In the context of ID, ML can be used to develop algorithms that automatically identify malicious activities and detect network intrusions. Machine learning techniques work by training models on large amounts of historical data and using these models to predict the likelihood of new events being benign or malicious. AI intrusion detection focuses on identifying unauthorized access and malicious activities within a network or system. On the other hand, anomaly detection aims to identify unusual patterns or behaviors that deviate from the norm. An intrusion detection rule describes a traffic anomaly that could be a sign of an attack in the industrial network. The rules contain the conditions that the intrusion detection system uses to analyze traffic. Intrusion detection rules are stored on the server and sensors. By detecting patterns and anomalies, even without known threat signatures, AI empowers organizations to swiftly identify and respond to potential security breaches. Moreover, AI excels at detecting potential insider threats through a comprehensive analysis of user activity across multiple systems and applications. AI content detectors use machine learning and natural language processing to inspect linguistic patterns and sentence structures to find out if it's AI-generated or human-written. It can detect unknown or emerging threats by identifying deviations from standard baselines of what is considered normal. Advanced AI algorithms, such as deep learning and neural networks, can analyze vast data sets for suspicious patterns, using existing intelligence to improve their predictive capabilities over time. By detecting and preventing security threats, such as cyberattacks and fraud, AI enhances network security and protection of users' data. AI algorithms can also be used for fraud detection and prevention in areas like billing and subscriber management, helping CSPs reduce losses and improve their financial performance. After all, AI algorithms can detect software identify patterns and spot basic viruses or ransomware attacks before they infiltrate computer systems. By leveraging natural language processing, AI enhances its capabilities and safeguards data by analyzing articles, news updates and cyber-risk research. AI security is the process of using AI to enhance an organization's security posture. With AI systems, organizations can automate threat detection, prevention and remediation to better combat cyberattacks and data breaches. ZeroGPT AI Content Detector has claims of high accuracy, but in tests, Originality AI is the most reliable AI content detector. The tool is easy to use and provides customers with clear results to improve their work. Object detection is a key field in artificial intelligence, allowing computer systems to see their environments by detecting objects in visual images or videos, whereas AI detectors try to find text that looks like it was generated by an AI writing tool. They do this by measuring specific characteristics of the text of perplexity that not by comparing it to a database. Plagiarism checkers try to find text that is copied from a different source. AI tools analyze network traffic in real-time, optimizing the flow to ensure smooth operation. This is particularly beneficial for enterprises with high data traffic, where efficient traffic management is key to preventing bottlenecks and ensuring fast, reliable access to resources. AI-powered risk analysis can produce incident summaries for high-fidelity alerts and automate incident responses, accelerating alert investigations and triage by an average of 55%. AI technology also helps identify vulnerabilities across threat landscapes and defends against cybercriminals and cybercrime.

Blockchain security is a comprehensive risk management system for a blockchain network. It uses cybersecurity frameworks, assurance services and best practices to reduce risks against attacks and fraud. An IPS is similar to an intrusion detection system but differs in that an IPS can be configured to block potential threats. Blockchain provides a secure method for storing data across a distributed network. This decentralization ensures that data is not stored in a single location, reducing the risk of data breaches and unauthorized access. Blockchain is a shared, immutable ledger that facilitates the process of recording transactions and tracking assets in a business network.

Employee training is one of the most effective network security protection measures that organizations can take to ensure that everyone who has access to the organization's network is trained not to inadvertently jeopardize the network's security. In addition, most people think about locks, bars, alarms and uniformed guards when they think about security. While these countermeasures are by no means the only precautions that need to be considered when trying to secure an information system, they are a perfectly logical place to begin. Finally, security measures enhance safety, prevent incidents, protect property and contribute to the overall well-being of individuals and communities. Let's appreciate the efforts of security professionals and work together to create a secure and harmonious society for everyone to thrive in.

6.4 Incident Response and Management Procedures

Incident management is the process used by development and IT operations teams to respond to an unplanned event or service interruption and restore the service to its operational state. The seven steps of incident response are Preparation, Identification, Containment, Eradication, Recovery, Learning and Re-testing. Incident response is a structured process organizations use to identify and deal with cybersecurity incidents.

The four Rs of incident management are Repair, Resolution, Recovery and Restoration and are the four Rs mostly used during the Incident Management process. While ITIL is very particular about the terms and terminology, there seems to be enough confusion while discussing these four terms. Incident response (IR) is the process by which an organization handles a data breach

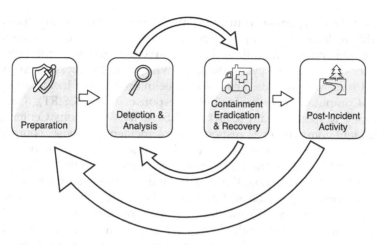

FIGURE 6.5
Incident response.

or cyberattack. It is an effort to quickly identify an attack, minimize its effects, contain damage and remediate the cause to reduce the risk of future incidents (Figure 6.5). The NIST incident response lifecycle breaks incident response down into four main phases: Preparation; Detection and Analysis; Containment, Eradication and Recovery; and Post-Event Activity. An Incident Response Policy is a critical document that outlines the structured approach an organization follows when responding to and managing a cybersecurity incident. Priority 1 (P1)—A complete business-down situation or single critical system down with high financial impact. The client is unable to operate. Priority 2 (P2)—A major component of the clients' ability to operate is affected. Some aspects of the business can continue, but it's a major problem. ITIL incident management (IM) is the practice of restoring services as quickly as possible after an incident, and it's a main component of ITIL service support. ITIL incident management is a reactive process. However, using IM to diagnose and escalate procedures to restore service is not a proactive measure. Based on the responsibilities, skills and qualities of an incident manager, we can define their role as follows: An incident manager is the leader and coordinator of the incident response team, who oversees the entire process of identifying, containing, analyzing and recovering from security breaches or cyberattacks. The five categories of incidents are: task, material, environment, personnel and management. When this model is used, possible causes in each category should be investigated. Each category is examined more closely in the following. Consequently, an incident handling checklist is a cybersecurity lifeline. It outlines a set of steps and key components to follow in the event of a security breach or incident. Each stage, from preparation to post-incident analysis, is integral to ensure a timely and thorough response. However, an SOC incident response process is a set of procedures and guidelines that defines how the SOC team handles different types of security events, from identification to remediation. An Incident Response Plan prepares a business for responding to a security breach or cyberattack. It outlines the steps an organization should take when they discover a potential cyberattack, allowing them to quickly identify, contain and remediate threats. There are three main types of incident response teams—Computer Security Incident Response Team (CSIRT), Computer Emergency Response Team (CERT) and Security Operations Center (SOC). The incident commander is responsible for incident response, coordinating and directing the response effort. A technical lead, often a senior technical responder, will analyze the issue, make decisions and manage the technical team. This plan details how the incident will be managed from occurrence to back-to-normal operation and provides information about the structure of the Incident Management Team, the criteria for invoking Business Continuity, the management of the incident, resource requirements and any necessary staff movements. Incident objectives, strategies and tactics are three fundamental pieces of a successful incident response. Incident objectives state what will be accomplished. Strategies establish the general plan or direction for accomplishing the incident objectives. Tactics specify how the strategies will be executed. These phases are defined in NIST SP 800-61 (Computer Security Incident Handling Guide). The initial phase involves establishing and training an incident response team and acquiring the necessary tools and resources. During preparation, the organization also attempts to limit the number of incidents that will occur by selecting and implementing a set of controls based on the results of risk assessments. An SLA is an agreement between you and your customer that defines how your relationship will work in the future. Key performance indicators (KPIs) are the metrics chosen to gauge how well a team performed against agreed-upon standards. As a result, the Response SLA is calculated from the time the incident is created and assigned to a group till it is assigned to someone from the group. It is the time taken to acknowledge the ticket. Resolution: Resolution SLA is calculated from the time the incident is created till the time the incident is resolved.

6.5 Privacy by Design

The term "Privacy by design" means nothing more than "data protection through technology design." Behind this is the thought that data protection in data processing procedures is best adhered to when it is already integrated in the technology when created. "Privacy by design" is a process for embedding good privacy practices into the design specifications of technologies, business practices and physical infrastructures. This means building privacy into the design specifications and architecture of new systems and processes. Some examples of Privacy by Design include:

Conducting a Data Protection Impact Assessment (DPIA) before using personal information in any way.

Providing the contact details of your Data Protection Officer (DPO) or other responsible party. Writing a Privacy Policy that's easy to read and kept up-to-date.

Some benefits of Privacy by design include the fact that it simply makes data protection in an organization stronger and thus data breaches less likely. Data breaches can lead to great monetary losses. That showing customers would be conscious about using data ethically, and that showing value and care about their privacy. Most data protection laws do not yet include provisions for privacy by design. Many countries, however, promote it as one of the most recommended practices for protecting online privacy. It has been recommended, for example, by the US Federal Trade Commission (FTC) and Canada's Privacy Commissioner. A privacy-first approach allows marketers to access the data they need to make insightful decisions but bakes in data privacy principles throughout the marketing process.

The five principles of design are: balance, contrast, alignment, hierarchy and repetition. These principles serve as the foundation for creating designs that are not only visually appealing but also functional. The privacy principles are defined as "a comprehensive and fundamental law, doctrine, or assumption." Privacy principles are therefore the underlying doctrine and rules that we follow in handling personal information. The new and emerging technologies argue for an expansion to the seven different types of privacy, including privacy of the person, privacy of behavior and action, privacy of personal communication, privacy of data and image, privacy of thoughts and feelings, privacy of location and space. Consequently, data privacy means empowering your users to make their own decisions about who can process their data and for what purpose. The following is a summary of the GDPR data privacy requirements. It may be helpful to first check out our GDPR overview to understand the GDPR's general structure and some of its key terms. Furthermore, privacy by design (PbD) is a proactive approach to protecting personal information, while data protection by design (DPbD) focuses on the technical and organizational measures needed to protect data from unauthorized access or misuse. However, privacy is a crucial concern for any web designer who works with clients and users' data and who has a responsibility to protect their personal information, preferences and behavior from unauthorized access, misuse or breach. The core privacy principle is: lawfulness, fairness and transparency.

However, in privacy by design user limitations option of collection, processing, and storage data as well as minimization and accuracy of data. The purpose of a Privacy Risk Assessment is to provide an early warning system to detect privacy problems, enhance the information available internally to facilitate informed decision-making, avoid costly or embarrassing mistakes in privacy compliance and provide evidence that an organization is attempting to minimize the risk. In the context of digital privacy, communication privacy is the notion that individuals should have the freedom, or right, to communicate information digitally with the expectation that their communications are secure—meaning that messages and communications will only be accessible to the sender's original intended recipient. Data privacy generally means the ability of a person to determine for themselves when, how and to what extent personal information about them is shared with or communicated to others. This personal information can be one's name, location, contact information or online or real-world behavior. Most data protection laws do not yet include provisions for privacy by design. Privacy of Body means that your body is your own, and governmental agents may not examine or invade it without your consent. Privacy is inherently an ethical concept that is understood to represent something other than an individual's obligation to show and tell all. In this sense, the private also implies the secret, which an individual may share at his or her discretion with a select few, rather than with society as a whole.

7

Privacy in Practice

Integrating Privacy by Design and Vendor Management

7.1 Principles of Privacy by Design

Privacy by design seeks to deliver the maximum degree of privacy by ensuring that personal data are automatically protected in any given IT system or business practice. If an individual does nothing, their privacy remains intact. Privacy by design measures are designed to anticipate and prevent privacy invasive events before they occur.

Privacy by design is a method of planning and implementing a system and architecture that fully supports individual rights and protects people's data. Developers are tasked with taking all privacy considerations into account as part of the development process. "Secure by design" means that technology products are built in a way that reasonably protects against malicious cyberactors successfully gaining access to devices, data, and connected infrastructure software. Microsoft is a prime example of a company that uses Security by Design principles. The company developed its own Security Development Lifecycle (SDL), a software process that embeds security requirements into every phase of the development process. "Secure by design" in software engineering means that software products and capabilities have been designed to be foundationally secure. Embedded security is complex and expensive. As the joint advisory points out, secure-by-design development requires the investment of significant resources by software manufacturers at each layer of the product design and development process which cannot be bolted on later. This means anticipating privacy-invasive events or scenarios before they occur and designing appropriate defenses against them. Closely related is the concept of making privacy the default setting in a system rather than requiring users to take action to enable privacy controls. AI privacy is the set of practices and concerns centered around the ethical collection, storage and usage of personal information by artificial intelligence systems. Individuals can minimize AI privacy risks by using strong passwords and implementing

DOI: 10.1201/9781003604679-7

multi-factor authentication. AI tools can potentially make it easier to hack weak passwords. As a result, people need to be diligent about protecting account access. For example, generative AI tools trained with data scraped from the internet may memorize personal information about people, as well as relational data about their family and friends. This data helps enable spear-phishing, the deliberate targeting of people for purposes of identity theft or fraud.

Be clear, open and honest with people from the start about how and why to use their personal data. That will indicate what explanation is needed in the context in which your AI system will be deployed. Privacy-preserving AI refers to the components of artificial intelligence that ensure the safety and anonymity of data during AI processes. It embodies the concepts of privacy and security within the machine learning models. Though AI makes failure to inform or give control to users over how their data is used worse through opaque data practices. Insecurity of AI's data requirements and storage practices risks data leaks and improper access, and exposure of AI can reveal sensitive information, such as through generative AI techniques. Developers must build AI algorithms that minimize the acquisition and processing of personal data while ensuring robust data security and confidentiality measures. This approach aims to strike a balance between providing personalized experiences and safeguarding user privacy. Users should know when their data is being used, whether AI is being used to make decisions about them and whether their data is being used in the creation of AI. They should also be given a choice to consent to such data use. A staggering 85 percent of AI projects fail. Several factors contribute to this high failure rate, including poor data quality, lack of relevant data and insufficient understanding of AI's capabilities and requirements. The main privacy concerns surrounding AI are the potential for data breaches and unauthorized access to personal information. With so much data being collected and processed, there is a risk that it could fall into the wrong hands, either through hacking or other security breaches. AI safety focuses on preventing unintended harm or negative consequences to humans, while AI security aims to protect AI systems from malicious attacks, data breaches and unauthorized access.

Ethical Considerations: Both domains involve ethical considerations related to the development and deployment of AI systems. Internet of Things privacy is the special considerations required to protect individuals' information from exposure in the IoT environment.

Anticipate, identify and prevent privacy invasive events before they occur. Build in the maximum degree of privacy into the default settings for any system or business practice. Some examples of privacy by design are:

- Minimizing the processing of personal data.
- Pseudonymizing personal data as soon as possible.
- Ensuring transparency in regard to the functions and processing of personal data.

- Enabling individuals to monitor the processing.
- Creating (and improving) security features.

Privacy by design is a concept that integrates privacy into the creation and operation of new devices, IT systems, networked infrastructure and even corporate policies. It's a UX designer's a job to make sure the designs consider and take full advantage of the unique features of each platform. When preparing a cross-platform design, it's helpful to keep the 4Cs in mind: Consistency, Continuity, Context and Complementarity.

Some benefits of privacy by design: It simply makes data protection in organization stronger and thus data breaches less likely. Data breaches can lead to great monetary losses. It shows customers that you are conscious about using data ethically, and that you value and care about their privacy. If a company handles personal data, it's important to understand and comply with the seven principles of the GDPR: Lawfulness, Fairness and Transparency; Purpose Limitation; Data Minimization; Accuracy; Storage Limitations; Integrity and Confidentiality; and Accountability.

Privacy by design is a holistic approach to privacy that encompasses some basic foundational principles: Proactive, not Reactive; Preventative, not Remedial; Privacy as the Default Setting; Privacy Embedded into Design. Furthermore, it develops six principles for guiding system design, based on a set of fair information practices common in most privacy legislation in use today: notice, choice and consent, proximity and locality, anonymity and pseudonymity, security, and access and recourse. Here are some ways to implement privacy by design in business:

- Take a "privacy-first" stance.
- Audit and map all personal data.
- Anonymize personal data.
- Implement security controls.
- Have agreements with third parties.
- Implement additional provisions for sensitive data.
- Empower users to exercise their rights.

Examples of privacy include—physical privacy (for instance, being frisked at airport security or giving a bodily sample for medical reasons); surveillance (where identity can't be proved or information isn't recorded); information privacy (how personal information is handled). A privacy model is a set of rules and assumptions that determine how an algorithm handles and protects personal or sensitive information, and what level of privacy it offers against threats such as surveillance, profiling or discrimination. Common privacy models include anonymity, pseudonymity and confidentiality. In addition, an effective design centers on four basic principles: contrast, repetition, alignment and proximity. This chapter provides a brief overview of the basic principles discussed in this text.

Privacy ethics are important because they play an important role in upholding human dignity and sustaining a strong and vibrant society. Respecting privacy is an essential part of what it means to be a good citizen, whether as an individual or as an institution. The goal of data privacy is to protect the means by which personal information is collected, stored and used. By extension, privacy controls are meant to ensure individuals have rights to control how their data is used, and to mitigate threats of unauthorized access, malicious actors and other potential risks.

There are 12 basic principles of design: contrast, balance, emphasis, proportion, hierarchy, repetition, rhythm, pattern, white space, movement, variety and unity. These visual and graphic design principles work together to create appealing and functional designs that make sense to users. Finally, the more common view is that privacy is valuable because it facilitates or promotes other fundamental values, including ideals of personhood such as personal autonomy (the ability to make personal decisions), individuality and respect.

7.2 Incorporating Privacy into Product and System Development

Integrating privacy practices with security practices and with the software development lifecycle helps minimize the overhead for developers, giving them a single process where this is all defined. Security and privacy practices address the obligations that a company takes on when they collect and use personal data. Key considerations for data privacy in software development are data collection and consent. Only collect data that is necessary for the software's functionality. Obtain clear and informed consent from users before gathering any information. Data Storage: Ensure data is stored securely.

It is important for developers to consider the privacy of its users; when users entrust companies with their data, the company is promising that it will respect their privacy and protect their information. When following through on this promise, customers will trust the policy and the company's reputation will reflect that. The key consideration for data privacy in software development is to only collect data that is necessary for the software's functionality. Obtain clear and informed consent from users before gathering any information. For data storage, ensure data is stored securely. A good way to start is to understand what customers want in terms of data privacy, including transparency, security and portability, along with clear communication and a solid understanding of their rights. Software development teams should be considering these business needs when developing software applications, since it relates to an individual's ability to determine for themselves when, how and for what purpose their personal information is handled by others.

Protecting privacy is key to ensuring human dignity, safety and self-determination. It allows individuals to freely develop their own personality. Privacy tools can help people control the information that they share with others. They are also known as privacy software, privacy apps and privacy utilities. Hence, privacy is not just about confidentiality but is also about having control over our own domains and knowledge about what is done with those domains. Privacy is integral to free speech, openness in research and the ethical treatment of individuals and institutional assets. Beyond compliance with laws, privacy is a trust.

Both privacy and security are equally important aspects of cyber-safety. Privacy rights should take measures to secure personal information and data within the digital environment. After all, privacy is a fundamental human right that is vital in the context of computer ethics. Privacy software, also called a privacy platform, is software built to protect the privacy of its users. The software typically works in conjunction with Internet usage to control or limit the amount of information made available to third parties. The software can apply encryption or filtering of various kinds. Furthermore, when users entrust an organization with their data, that organization is promising to them that it will respect their privacy and protect their information. By following through on this promise, customers will trust the organization, and its reputation will reflect that.

Software security is critical because a malware attack can cause extreme damage to any piece of software while compromising integrity, authentication and availability. If programmers take this into account in the programming stage, not afterward, damage can be stopped before it begins. As a result, the key factors of software security are: Confidentiality, Authenticity, Integrity, Utility, Availability, Possession, Availability, Authentication, Authorization, Non-repudiation, Tamper-proofness, Unavoidability, Verifiability, Privacy, Reliability, Safety, Maintainability, Access Control and Resource Access.

7.3 Role of Privacy Impact Assessments

A privacy impact assessment (PIA) is an analysis of how personally identifiable information (PII) is handled to ensure compliance with appropriate regulations, determine the privacy risks associated with information systems or activities and evaluate ways to reduce the privacy risks. The Privacy Impact Assessment (PIA) describes a process used to evaluate the collection of personal data in information systems.

Impact analysis assesses the potential consequences of cyber threats, aiding businesses in understanding risks to their operations and reputation.

This process is crucial for prioritizing cybersecurity responses and allocating resources effectively. A PIA assists organizations in meeting compliance and regulatory requirements related to cybersecurity. By assessing the potential impacts of cyber incidents, organizations can align their security measures with industry standards and regulations. The PIA enables early detection of an improper balance in your body composition, which allows earlier intervention and prevention. PIA also provides the measurement of fluid and body mass that can be a critical assessment tool for your current state of health.

AI technology promises significant benefits for businesses, including improved customer engagement, data analysis, automation of processes, strategic recommendations and enhanced decision-making. With AI-powered data analysis, businesses gain a deeper understanding of their customers, markets and industry dynamics. This data-driven approach empowers decision-makers to make well-informed decisions promptly, minimizing risks and optimizing opportunities. AI enhances decision-making by leveraging vast data to identify patterns and trends often invisible to humans. Machine learning algorithms can analyze historical data and predict future outcomes, allowing businesses and individuals to make informed decisions quickly and accurately. Organizations use AI to strengthen data analysis and decision-making, improve customer experiences, generate content, optimize IT operations, sales, marketing and cybersecurity practices and more. As AI technologies improve and evolve, new business applications emerge. Amazon is the king of e-commerce AI. Whether it's the company's recommendations on which products to buy, the warehouse robots that grab, sort and ship products or the web services that power the website itself, Amazon employs AI in almost every step of its process. For example, Sisense is considered one of the best AI tools for business analytics because of its drop-down interface and developer-friendly features. Sisense solves business analytics problems using natural language processing and generative AI.

Furthermore, AI data analytics is designed to support, automate and simplify each stage of the data analysis journey. AI tools can help with data collection, ingesting from multiple sources and preparation, cleaning and organizing for analysis. Hence, good BAs can communicate and understand user feelings and challenges and how those integrate with solutions and technology better than AI can assess. AI is a great tool to assist BAs, but if a BA can be replaced by AI, they're not doing a uniquely good job. However, AI may have positive impacts on productivity and democratization of skills. Several studies have suggested AI may be beneficial for worker productivity across tasks like business writing, programming, customer support and consulting. Research shows that AI can help less experienced workers enhance their productivity more quickly. Younger workers may find it easier to exploit opportunities, while older workers could struggle to adapt. The effect on labor income will largely depend on the extent to which AI will complement high-income workers. In the finance industry, AI technology has already proven integral in fraud detection, automated trading and streamlining processes, among other capabilities. The efficiency and decision-making improvements brought about by AI in finance are undeniable. AI brings multiple benefits to businesses: better efficiency, sharper decision-making, personalized customer experiences and turbocharged innovation. AI technology can also identify trends, patterns and anomalies that humans might find impossible to discern. Data overload can be solved by AI software, which allows businesses to make data-driven decisions, improve customer targeting and enhance product development. Many companies have incorporated AI technology into their consumer-facing software platforms to provide a more personalized experience. AI can analyze a consumer's past behavior and use that information to provide unique individualized recommendations. This helps improve customer engagement and builds brand loyalty. AI also offers personalized customer interactions, sentiment analysis tools and predictive analytics. All of these tools transform customer service and create an optimal customer journey, which in turn can benefit sales and lead conversion rates. Blockchain improves customer engagement by bringing access, transparency, simplification and trust to business processes. The combination of blockchain and customer engagement creates numerous opportunities and benefits. In marketing, blockchain can be used to increase the security and transparency around the sharing of customer data, either between a customer and a company or between two companies. Blockchain can also be used to reduce fraud and other trust-related issues in digital ad buying. Blockchain can digitize the entire trade finance lifecycle with increased security and efficiency. It can enable more transparent governance, decreased processing times, lower capital requirements and reduced risks of fraud, human error and overall counterparty risk. New business models in blockchain can enable the creation of potentially lucrative and innovative business models. Blockchain could potentially lower expenses and boost productivity across various real-life processes. After all, blockchain offers significant advancements in credit assessments and the reduction of bad loans. By facilitating the sharing of verified customer data among participating banks, it simplifies processes such as syndicated lending, thereby reducing redundancy and accelerating operations. Hence, blockchain applications go far beyond cryptocurrency and Bitcoin. With its ability to create more transparency and fairness while also saving businesses time and money, the technology is impacting a variety of sectors in ways that range from how contracts are enforced to making governments work more efficiently. Blockchain's innate transparency builds trust among stakeholders at every step of the manufacturing process, from raw material procurement to shop floor operations to distributors of the finished product to customers. It can improve processes like drafting and enforcing contracts and supply chain monitoring. Improved financial reporting such as real-time data access enhances reporting accuracy. A study by Accenture found that blockchain can reduce reporting errors by 67%. Blockchain's security features deter fraudulent activities. Benefits of blockchain for business process management can lead to trust in the integrity and accuracy of the data within. Any party on the network can verify that the right processes are being followed, and smart contracts can even enforce adherence to these processes. Furthermore, the purpose of the PIA is to identify and prioritize system components by correlating them to the mission of business process the system supports, and using this information to characterize the impact on the processes if the system were unavailable.

Big data, by contrast, captures minute customer actions, allowing businesses to create more targeted marketing campaigns based on that data. Big data analysis may not always be perfect, but it is highly accurate. This high accuracy allows companies to target marketing to perceived customer needs. Big data describes large and diverse datasets that are huge in volume and rapidly grow in size over time. Big data is used in machine learning, predictive modeling and other advanced analytics to solve business problems and make informed decisions. Business operations, such as business activity of all kinds, can be improved by using big data. It helps optimize business processes to generate cost savings, boost productivity and increase customer satisfaction. Hiring and HR management can become more effective. A big data strategy helps your organization use big data efficiently. If we consider big data as an economic resource, similar in nature to other assets, defining a big data strategy is a logical step. Big data analytics is important because it lets organizations use colossal amounts of data in multiple formats from multiple sources to identify opportunities and risks, helping organizations move quickly to improve their bottom lines. For example, analysis of big data on a company's energy use can help it be more efficient. Big data can be used to identify solvable problems, such as improving healthcare or tackling poverty in a certain area.

The objectives of a PIA are to determine if collected personal information data is necessary and relevant, to systematically identify the risks and potential effects of collecting, maintaining and disseminating PII and to examine and evaluate alternative processes for handling information to mitigate potential privacy risks. Other objectives PIA include providing a tool to make informed policy and system design or procurement decisions based on an understanding of privacy risks and options available for mitigating these risks and ensuring that system and program managers are accountable for the proper handling of privacy issues. Benefits of conducting a PIA may include: The confirmation of the legal authority for the project to collect, use, retain and disclose personal information, and the ability to demonstrate due diligence and evidence of compliance needed to support informed decision-making during the development of the project. To implement a privacy impact assessment:

- Determine the need for a PIA in a project.
- Plan and scope the PIA.

- Identify and coordinate with all parties involved.
- Outline the informational flow.
- Conduct privacy risk and compliance checks.
- Identify possible strategies to mitigate identified risks.

A Privacy Impact Assessment is an analysis of how personally identifiable information is handled in DOD information systems or electronic collections. The PIA examines and evaluates protections for handling information to mitigate potential privacy risks. When creating a new program, system, technology, or any form of information collection that could be privacy implications. The same concern applies when updating a system which could introduce new privacy risks. Therefore, it is important to conduct a privacy impact assessment (PIA) or data protection impact assessment (DPIA). These assessments are required when issuing new or updated rules that involve the collection of personally identifiable information (PII). The requirement for these assessments was introduced with the General Data Protection Regulation (GDPR). A PIA should be undertaken early enough in the development of a project so that its findings can influence the project's design. This will prevent unnecessary effort being expended on design options that are not compliant with the IP Act. A PIA is also a risk management process that helps institutions ensure they meet legislative requirements and identifies the impacts their programs and activities will have on individuals' privacy. As a general rule, a PIA is required when the proposed processing activity presents a heightened risk to the privacy of individuals. This can include activities such as when new or novel technologies are present, monitoring consumer behavior or making significant changes to existing systems. These events also constitute triggers for an organization to conduct a privacy impact assessment: Conversion of records from paper-based to electronic form; Conversion of information from anonymous to identifiable form; System management changes involving significant new uses and/or application of new technologies. Data Protection Impact Assessment (DPIA) is all about identifying and minimizing risks associated with the processing of personal data. Consequently, the point of a Privacy Impact Assessment is to determine if systems, and the organizations that manage them, comply with all federal laws, regulations and security policies. Threats to privacy and mitigating factors should also be noted in a PIA. Furthermore, it should analyze potential threats and vulnerabilities that put data at risk given its sensitivity levels and obligations, including: Cyber threats like malware, ransomware, insider and third-party breaches; System failures, outages or data corruption; Improper access controls or retention policies. As a result, a privacy impact assessment is a method for identifying and assessing privacy risks throughout the development lifecycle of a program or system. These assessments state what personally identifiable information is collected and explain how that information is maintained, protected and shared.

7.4 Vendor Management and Third-Party Risk

Vendor Risk Management (VRM) is the act of identifying and addressing any type of risk that is associated with vendor entities. A vendor is third-party entity that provides a product or service directly to you. All vendors are third parties, but not all third parties are vendors. As the names and definitions suggest, VRM focuses on vendors, while TPRM manages the risk of all kinds of third parties. VRM VRM gives companies visibility into the vendors they work with and how they work with them, and which vendors have implemented sufficient security controls. Third-Party Risk Management (TPRM) is the process of analyzing and minimizing risks associated with outsourcing to third-party vendors or service providers. There are many types of digital risks within the third-party risk category. These could include financial, environmental, reputational and security risks. A vendor/third-party risk management process is, at its core, a guiding framework allowing organizations to conduct thorough due diligence during the vendor selection process. It also ensures the ongoing monitoring of current vendors on a periodic or continuous basis.

A third-party is the most exhaustive term, meaning any entity connected to the institution, independent of a contract's existence. A vendor is a subset of a third-party, including those entities with whom the institution has a contract or conducts commerce. Risk management in cybersecurity is the practice of identifying and minimizing potential risks or threats to networked systems, data and users. Through the security vendor, Ledger SAS, and any other individuals or entities engaged from time to time to provide security, custodian, or related services to the Trust, do so under the authority delegated by the sponsor. Vendor relationship management is focused on overseeing the relationship with vendors, from due diligence and cybersecurity risk assessment through the delivery of the goods or services to planning for business continuity (Figure 7.1). Research indicates there are more than 3200 cybersecurity vendors, and the list is constantly changing through new launches, acquisitions and the inevitable failure of many of these VC-funded pipe dreams.

Engaging third-party vendors for the provision of goods and services is not a new concept. Vendor risk management is important because managing vendor risk is foundational to cybersecurity, ensuring business continuity and maintaining regulatory compliance. Vendor cybersecurity protects organization by ensuring that vendors, suppliers and third-party partners are protecting their information systems, data and networks from cyber threats. IoT solution providers typically offer various services, including hardware design and manufacturing, software development, cloud hosting and management, data analytics and consulting services. A vendor is the last entity in the chain that brands a product and sells it directly to end users or through a channel. A vendor may design and manufacture its own products, assemble complete systems from components produced by others or procure

Vendor and Third-Party Risk Management

FIGURE 7.1
Vendor Risk Management (VRM).

products from an original equipment or contract manufacturer. Vendors can operate online or through a physical storefront, and they may offer a broad range of products or specialize in specific categories. Blockchain vendors are companies that provide services to other startups or businesses aiming to use blockchain. Clearly, not every company can create an end-to-end solution. Also, the wide range of use cases for blockchain means a different approach every single time a problem needs to be solved. The vendor, or seller, is the individual or entity that legally owns the property and is looking to transfer ownership to a purchaser. The vendor's responsibilities are extensive and primarily focused on ensuring that the property is legally and physically ready for sale. A crypto broker is a firm or an individual who acts as a financial intermediary for persons who want to exchange their fiat money for cryptocurrencies. A cryptocurrency broker, like Bitpanda, provides online financial services for users who want to buy or sell cryptocurrencies and other assets. Currently, over 15,000 businesses worldwide accept Bitcoin, including about 2,300 companies in the United States. Most crypto-friendly companies are small businesses, and shoppers may not think to ask if they take Bitcoin. Vendor intelligence suites enrich third-party risk management processes with targeted risk intelligence that informs the onboarding and management of third parties throughout the entire vendor lifecycle. A software vendor, also known as an independent software vendor (ISV), is a company that develops, produces and sells software. Software vendors sell their products directly or indirectly to customers through several channels, such as application marketplaces. A vendor code is a unique identifier that a company assigns to a vendor in its system. Each organization may have a different name for a vendor code, such as supplier code or Vendor ID, but the purpose is the same. Organizations collect various data points in procurement, including supplier performance data, purchase order data, invoice data and market data. They collect this data through various means, including ERP systems, procurement software and external sources. Microsoft SQL Server is a popular SQL vendor that offers a range of data management and business intelligence tools. SQL Server is known for its ease of use, and it offers a wide range of features, including analytics, reporting and data warehousing.

Furthermore, "third-party" is a catch-all term used to describe every organization your company interacts with, while "vendor" is typically used to describe a provider of a product or service. Hence, the different types of vendor risks are:

- Cybersecurity risk.
- Information security risk.
- Compliance risk.
- Environmental, social and governance (ESG) risks.
- Reputational risk.
- Financial risk.
- Operational risk.
- Strategic risk.

This process will involve your legal team:

Create documentation of the vendor selection process and criteria, available vendor details and audit reports of each review taking place at the vendor site.

Conduct a periodic review and audit of clauses included within the contract.

Ensure they are met.

Third-party risk is any risk brought into an organization by external parties in its ecosystem or supply chain. Such parties may include vendors, suppliers, partners, contractors or service providers who have access to internal company or customer data, systems, processes or other privileged information. A vendor risk management program reduces the frequency and severity of data breaches, data leaks and cyberattacks involving third and fourth parties, protecting sensitive data, PII, PHI, intellectual property and ensuring business continuity. It helps evaluate risks posed to an entire supply chain through third-party vendors and services that can lead to reputational damage, monetary penalties, financial loss and cost the organization time and resources. An example of this would be hiring a cleaning service to come to your place of business and provide janitorial services vs purchasing cleaning supplies for in-house janitorial staff. Choosing between these options may be part of vendor management. A third-party vendor is any entity that your organization does business with. This includes suppliers, manufacturers, service providers, business partners, affiliates, brokers, distributors, resellers and agents. A third-party vendor provides services for another company (or that company's customers). While vendors are considered "third parties," some industries differentiate a "third-party vendor" specifically as a vendor under written contract, but not all vendors work under a contract. Consequently, to maintain high standards of efficiency, supply chains everywhere need products and services from third-party vendors. Maintaining relationships with suppliers is a well-accepted part of keeping up production lines, controlling internal operations and generally conducting business. Furthermore, the purpose of this policy is to ensure that all vendors have appropriate controls to minimize risks that could adversely impact confidentiality, availability and/or integrity of the service or product. Second, vendor risk management minimizes exposure to preventable risks if they are performing adequate due diligence on each critical and high-risk vendor. Third, it keeps things organized and less prone to missing key contract dates, like a non-renewal notice period or a vendor risk assessment expiration. To identify vendor risk you need to analyze company data: Research information about potential vendors using direct research, the internet and other research tools, business relationships and investment analysts; Perform due diligence by addressing the potential risks that you uncover and discuss them with the vendor. Ultimately, senior management and the board of directors are accountable for vendor risk management. Each person who deals with a vendor plays a significant part in making the wheels turn.

Vendor management includes activities such as selecting vendors, negotiating contracts, controlling costs, reducing vendor-related risks and ensuring service delivery (Figure 7.2). The vendor risk assessment (VRA), also known as vendor risk review, is the process of identifying and evaluating potential risks or hazards associated with a vendor's operations and products and their potential impact on your organization. The lifecycle of vendor risk management, or third-party risk management lifecycle, is an easy-to-follow system that organizes these various activities into three distinct phases: onboarding, ongoing and offboarding. A vendor risk assessment matrix enables you to focus on the most impactful areas of the vendor risk assessment program by visualizing your vendor risks by security rating and level of criticality. A vendor management policy (VMP) is a structural control for identifying and prioritizing the vendors that put organization at risk. It helps your company minimize the risks associated with third-party and fourth-party vendors by defining security controls. A high-risk vendor is a third-party vendor with access to a company's sensitive corporate information, handling its financial transactions and having a high risk of information loss. A high-risk vendor is also a vendor that an organization depends on to run its operations. In addition, procurement and vendor management are often seen as two separate functions. However, they are actually closely linked. Procurement is the

FIGURE 7.2
Vendor risk and third-party.

process of acquiring goods or services from external suppliers, while vendor management is the process of managing relationships with those suppliers. Finally, a vendor management system is a tool that is used by the recruiting department of companies and by staffing agencies for managing the vendors or recruitment process partners.

8

Beyond Borders

Third-Party Security and Emerging Technologies

8.1 Assessing Third-Party Security Posture

A third-party risk assessment (also known as supplier risk assessment) quantifies the risks associated with third-party vendors and suppliers that provide products or services to an organization. This assessment is useful for analyzing both new and ongoing supplier relationships. A four-step process for conducting vendor and other third-party risk assessments can scale to companies of different sizes and industries.

- Develop vendor risk criteria.
- Create a preliminary vendor risk profile.
- Perform due diligence based on risk profile.
- Address the risks that are uncovered.

The three steps of security risk assessment are: determine scope—identify which parts of the organization and which systems need to be assessed. Threat and vulnerability identification—scanning the relevant systems to identify vulnerabilities and security weaknesses. Analyze risks—determine the business impact of each vulnerability if it were exploited. Third-party security is a set of practices, services and technologies that can identify risks and protect your organization from security threats associated with third-party vendors. Third-party risk management is becoming a critical part of any organization's information security strategy. A third-party risk assessment is an analysis of the risks introduced to your organization via third-party relationships along the supply chain. Those third parties can include vendors, service providers, software providers and other suppliers. It helps evaluate risks posed to your entire supply chain through third-party vendors and services that can lead to reputational damage, monetary penalties, financial loss and can cost your organization time and resources. It's a relationship that must

DOI: 10.1201/9781003604679-8

be managed throughout the third-party management (TPM) lifecycle, from screening to onboarding, assessment, risk mitigation, monitoring and off-boarding. Risk assessment evaluates the risks and acts to prevent them. This stage is about creating a safe work environment. Evaluate the likelihood and severity of risks, and then put precautions and control measures in place. The testing or evaluation of security controls determines the extent to which the controls are implemented correctly, operating as intended and producing the desired outcome with respect to meeting the security requirements for an information system or organization. The scope of a security assessment is documented in a Security Assessment Plan (SAP), which identifies the security controls and enhancements under assessment, describes the assessment procedures utilized to determine the security control effectiveness and outlines the assessment environment team. Consequently, a security risk assessment identifies, assesses, and implements key security controls in applications. It also focuses on preventing application security defects and vulnerabilities. Carrying out a risk assessment allows an organization to view the application portfolio holistically—from an attacker's perspective. Hence, third-party vulnerability is a security problem detected in the third-party libraries loaded in your environment. In addition, a third-party data breach is an incident where sensitive data not stolen directly from an organization, but through one of its third-party vendors. In this case, the vendor's systems are misused to access the organization's systems. Third-Party Risk Management (TPRM) is the process of analyzing and minimizing risks associated with outsourcing to third-party vendors or service providers. There are many types of digital risks within the third-party risk category. These could include financial, environmental, reputational and security risks. In third-party order processing, a company does not deliver the items requested by a customer, instead passing the order along to a third-party supplier who then ships the goods directly to the customer and bills them. A sales order may consist partly or wholly of third-party items. Third-party monitoring is the practice of continually gathering and analyzing externally observable data on vendor cybersecurity posture, business ethics, financial status and geopolitical context to identify potential supply chain risks. Third-party risk and compliance management software is how the platform helps organizations to effectively and efficiently manage the risk, cost and complexity of critical vendors throughout the entire relationship—onboarding, contracts, due diligence, performance monitoring, quality and service level management. Security assessments use a variety of techniques and tests to conduct an in-depth audit of your organization's defense measures against various attack methods used by intruders—internal or external. This could be an attacker targeting your network from the outside, a disgruntled employee seeking revenge or malware. For examples of third-party risk, if a software vendor is hacked, your organization could be left with a downed system. A supplier's inventory could be impacted by a natural disaster, leaving your

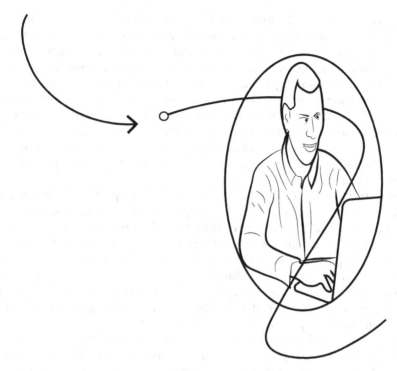

FIGURE 8.1
Third-party risk management.

own supply chain in chaos. Healthcare systems rely on hundreds of vendors to perform critical operations (Figure 8.1).

Because of the difficulties third parties face in gaining any representation, they tend to exist to promote a specific issue or personality. Often, the intent is to force national public attention on such an issue. Third-party standard means a standard for defining, reporting and assessing overall corporate social and environmental performance. Third-party features mean those features of the services and licensed software offered by third parties as identified on a sales agreement. Consequently, organizations can manage this risk through service level agreements (SLAs), and by setting up a backup vendor to ensure business continuity. Compliance risk—a third party can impact the organization's compliance with regulations, agreements or legislation, such as the EU's General Data Protection Regulation. Furthermore, third-party risk is any risk brought on to an organization by external parties in its ecosystem or supply chain. Such parties may include vendors, suppliers, partners, contractors or service providers who have access to internal company or customer data, systems, processes or other privileged information. Hence, third-party cyber-risk includes potential data breaches due to vulnerabilities within a vendor's IT environment and can lead to financial, reputational, and regulatory or compliance consequences. A security questionnaire is a set of questions designed to help an organization identify potential cybersecurity weaknesses among its third-party and fourth-party vendors, business partners and service providers. Organizations use security questionnaires to deliver informed vendor risk assessments. Application security risk assessment checklists can help organizations determine which areas of their application environment need additional protection or attention to ensure that their systems remain secure from malicious actors. Every application is unique and carries threat factors.

A security risk assessment is a process that helps organizations identify, analyze and implement security controls in the workplace. It prevents vulnerabilities and threats from infiltrating the organization and protects physical and informational assets from unauthorized users. The security assessment report provides visibility into specific weaknesses and deficiencies in the security controls employed within or inherited by the information system that could not reasonably be resolved during system development or that are discovered post-development. Security risk assessment is done by determining scope—identifying which parts of the organization and which systems need to be assessed. Threat and vulnerability identification—scanning the relevant systems to identify vulnerabilities and security weaknesses. Analyze risks—determine the business impact of each vulnerability if it were exploited. As a result, security risk management is the ongoing process of identifying these security risks and implementing plans to address them. Risk is determined by considering the likelihood that known threats will exploit vulnerabilities and the impact they have on valuable assets.

8.2 Contractual Obligations for Data Protection

Reasonable security arrangements have to be made to protect the personal data in your organization's possession to prevent unauthorized access, collection, use, disclosure or similar risks. Data protection agreements are used to protect personal information (PI) about customers when organizations are sharing information. There are two essential types of data security obligations: the duty to protect information and the duty to disclose breaches. The duty of security for data, systems and communications is to ensure the quality of data. Data protection is the process of protecting sensitive information from damage, loss or corruption. As the amount of data being created and stored has increased at an unprecedented rate, data protection has become increasingly important. The Security Council is one of the six main organs of the United Nations established under the UN Charter. Its primary responsibility is maintaining international peace and security. The Council has 5 permanent and 10 non-permanent members. The Council's powers include the establishment of peacekeeping and special political missions, authorization of military enforcement action, the imposition of international sanctions on member states and the ability to refer matters to the International Criminal Court (ICC). In general, cybersecurity focuses on protecting an organization's systems and networks against cyber threats, such as ransomware, phishing, etc. Cyber-protection brings an increased focus on data security, combining elements of cybersecurity and data protection. The 15-member UN Security Council seeks to address threats to international security. Its five permanent members, chosen in the wake of World War II, have veto power. The Security Council fosters negotiations, imposes sanctions and authorizes the use of force, including the deployment of peacekeeping missions.

In the context of AI, data protection considerations therefore must include the individuals whose personal data trains the system, and the impact the system has on the rights and freedoms of individuals and society once it is deployed. The GDPR stipulates that for any specific purpose, only the minimal required data should be used. AI mechanisms must abide by this, preventing the collection or manipulation of unnecessary data. In addition, data gathered for one aim should not be repurposed without additional consent. Through the role of AI in data security, AI systems are designed to continuously learn and adapt, allowing them to anticipate and respond to potential threats more efficiently. They can analyze vast quantities of data at an unprecedented speed, identifying patterns and anomalies that may indicate a security breach. One of the primary challenges is the potential for AI to be used to violate privacy. AI systems require vast amounts of personal data, and if this data falls into the wrong hands it can be used for nefarious purposes, such as identity theft or cyberbullying. AI is increasingly utilized in various security aspects to enhance threat detection, incident response and overall cybersecurity. Some key ways AI is used in security include advanced threat detection and anomaly detection. AI identifies unusual patterns indicating potential threats. While embracing data validation and leveraging human expertise are crucial, data cleaning remains the workhorse of ensuring high-quality data for AI. It's the process of identifying, rectifying and ultimately removing inconsistencies, errors and missing values from your data set. Furthermore, the AI Act is the first comprehensive worldwide legal framework on AI. The aim of the new rules is to foster trustworthy AI in Europe and beyond by ensuring that AI systems respect fundamental rights, safety and ethical principles and by addressing risks of very powerful and impactful AI models. For example, generative AI tools trained with data scraped from the internet may memorize personal information about people, as well as relational data about their family and friends. This data helps enable spear phishing, the deliberate targeting of people for purposes of identity theft or fraud. Data in AI applications is used for training machine learning models, making predictions and improving decision-making. Examples include facial recognition in surveillance systems, recommendation engines in e-commerce platforms and predictive maintenance in manufacturing. AI can automate data integration from different sources, formats and structures. ML models map and transform data, making it more consistent and analyzable. This is especially helpful in large organizations with a variety of data sources. Through its ability to proactively detect threats by analyzing data access patterns in real-time, AI can alert about suspicious behavior, such as attempted intrusions or unauthorized access. To take data governance even further, AI leverages machine-learning-based malware detection systems. One of the design features of blockchain architecture is that transaction records cannot be changed or deleted after the fact. A subsequent transaction can always annul the first transaction, but the first transaction will remain in the chain. The GDPR recognizes a right to ensure the data quality. In most blockchains or distributed ledger technologies, the data is structured into blocks and each block contains a transaction or bundle of transactions. Each new block connects to all the blocks before it in a cryptographic chain in such a way that it's nearly impossible to tamper with. Since blockchain uses strong encryption methods to keep data safe. Each transaction is turned into a secret code using special math, so only the right people can see it. This makes it extremely challenging for hackers to mess with the data, because they can't understand the secret code. Protecting data in transit necessitates defining the requirements and implementing controls, including encryption, and reduces the risk of unauthorized access or exposure. Providing the appropriate level of protection for data in transit protect the confidentiality and integrity of IoT data. Be sure to use strong passwords, multi-factor authentication and encryption for devices and applications. Manage both active and inactive devices, being sure to always patch the ones using and disconnect the system. The key requirements for any IoT security solution are device and data security, including authentication of devices, and confidentiality and integrity of data. Implementing and running security operations at IoT scale. Meeting compliance requirements and requests. IoT security is needed to help prevent data breaches because IoT devices transfer data over the internet unencrypted and operate undetected by standard cybersecurity systems. Data privacy defines who has access to data, while data protection provides tools and policies to actually restrict access to the data. Compliance regulations help ensure that users' privacy requests are carried out by companies, and companies are responsible for taking measures to protect private user data, even encrypting data into a code that's nearly impossible to decipher without the proper key. Ensure that your cloud provider uses robust encryption protocols, both in transit during transfer and at rest when stored. Although ISO 27018 is the pioneer international standard that deals with personal data protection in cloud computing, ISO/IEC 27018 establishes universally recognized control objectives and protocols. A number of different teams within an organization could be responsible for cloud security: the network team, security team, apps team, compliance team or the infrastructure team. However, cloud security is also a shared responsibility between the broader organization and its cloud vendor. Data privacy generally means a person's ability to determine for themselves when, how, and to what extent personal information about them is shared with or communicated to others. This personal information can be one's name, location, contact information, or online or real-world behavior. The responsibility here is a shared one, shared between the organization, the cloud provider and all its users. While data can be safe in the cloud, everyone with access to that data affects whether it remains safe. Cloud security must be everyone's responsibility.

Even if authorization is given, the processor must put in place a contract with the sub- processor. The terms of the contract must offer an equivalent level of protection for the personal data as those that exist in the contract between the controller and the processor. The seven principles of data protection are:

- Lawfulness, fairness and transparency.
- Purpose limitation.
- Data minimization.
- Accuracy.
- Storage limitation.
- Integrity and confidentiality (security).
- Accountability.

The protection obligation of PDPA companies ought to deploy required security measures to protect personal data they possess. This is to prevent third parties from having unauthorized access, collection, use and disclosure of personal data. Some of the most common types of data security, which organizations should combine to ensure they have the best possible strategy, include encryption, data erasure, data masking and data resiliency. A data contract defines the structure, format, semantics, quality and terms of use for exchanging data between a data provider and their consumers. A data contract is implemented by a data product's output port or other data technologies.

Whereas to protect personal data in its possession or under its control in order to prevent unauthorized access, collection, use, disclosure, copying, modification, disposal or similar risks. Article 5 of the UK GDPR sets out seven key principles which lie at the heart of the general data protection regime. Article 5(1) requires that personal data shall be: "(a) processed lawfully, fairly and in a transparent manner in relation to individuals ('lawfulness, fairness and transparency')." Furthermore, the material contractual obligations are those whose fulfillment is essential for the proper execution of the contract and whose observance may be relied on by the supplier. The

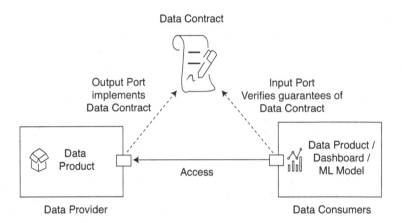

FIGURE 8.2
Security risk assessment.

main points of the Data Protection Act of 2018 are providing individuals with rights, including the right to know what information is held about them and the right to access that information. It states that anyone who processes personal information must comply with the principles in the Act. Meanwhile, compliance with PDPA rules is obligatory for organizations operating in Singapore (companies and unincorporated bodies) with respect to the collection, use and disclosure of personal data (Figure 8.2). There are four major data classification levels: public, internal, confidential and restricted. Data classification standards like GDPR, NIST 800-53 and ISO 27001 help businesses maintain data integrity and remain compliant with relevant industry regulations. The third principle requires that the personal data you are processing is adequate, relevant and not excessive. This means the data must be limited to what is necessary for the purposes are processing it. After all, part of the primary importance of data contracts is their role in ensuring data quality and integrity throughout the data lifecycle. By defining standards, formats and validation protocols for data exchange, contracts promote adherence to consistent data structures and quality benchmarks.

8.3 Monitoring and Auditing Third-Party Data Handling Practices

Third-party monitoring is about performing ongoing due diligence on external partners in order to protect the financial and information security of a business. Third-party monitoring ensures sustainability, trust and transparency in a vendor relationship. The following are some prominent examples

Security Risk Assessment

FIGURE 8.3
Contractual obligations for data protection.

What Is a Third-Party Processor?

FIGURE 8.4
Monitoring and auditing third-party data handling practices.

of where enhanced third-party monitoring could have helped organizations avoid problems.

A third-party audit is performed by an audit organization independent of the customer-supplier relationship and is free of any conflict of interest. Independence of the audit organization is a key component of a third-party audit (Figure 8.3). Third-party monitoring is important because it increases accountability. Third-party monitoring also ensures program management transparency, which helps promote trust in the program's objectives. Improved program delivery, such as appropriate feedback and reporting, guarantee that the program operates at optimal efficiency. The third-party processor is an individual or legal entity that processes personal data under the instructions of a data controller. This processor is in a direct relationship with the controller and acts in this controller's interest (Figure 8.4).

Third-party data can be described as data sets collected and managed by organizations that do not directly interact with customers or business data consumers. Third-party data can include data sets that are "stitched" together from a wide range of sources or even come from governmental, non-profit or academic sources. Third-party project monitoring is the process of tracking the progress and performance of external contractors or vendors working on a project. Third-party risk monitoring is the continuous assessment of third-party vendors who have entered into a business relationship with a company, to understand how much risk they pose to an organization at any given moment. Monitoring is critical to any third-party risk management program (TPRM). Third-party audits provide an objective assessment of a company's food safety and quality management systems. This ensures that companies are meeting the required standards and regulations set by government agencies and industry associations. The benefits of third-party audits are the validation. Third-party auditors validate existing programs and identify areas where best practices can be implemented to further protect the company. They assist in identifying issues before they become violations and determine root causes of continuing issues—focusing on corrective actions to be implemented. The most common types of audits are internal audit, external audit, tax audit, statutory audit and compliance audit. These auditing types are directly linked to business finances and detecting fraud in the firm. Effective risk monitoring of third parties involves conducting due diligence, establishing clear contracts, setting up ongoing monitoring processes, implementing controls, communicating with the third party and using risk assessment tools. Monitoring and evaluation are critical for understanding the effectiveness of any project or program. Regular assessment allows us to identify successes and areas where improvements can be made. It also ensures accountability, allowing stakeholders to track progress and hold each other responsible for achieving goals.

Third-party risk is the likelihood that your organization will experience an adverse event (e.g., data breach, operational disruption, reputational damage) when you choose to outsource certain services or use software built by third parties to accomplish certain tasks. Furthermore, first-party data is what is collected from the audience directly via your own channels. Third-party data is collected by another entity that is entirely separate from a relationship with the audience. So, these terms are about where data comes from—how it ends up in a marketer's hands. Third-party data is often generated on a variety of websites and platforms and is then aggregated together by a third-party data provider, such as a DMP. This means that a third-party data breach will involve an incident where personal data is compromised via a third-party vendor, rather than directly through an organization. The provider gathers this data from several businesses with no direct relationship with the customer. While third-party data helps us learn about current customers, it can also enable us to identify lookalike audiences composed of consumers who resemble the customer base. That can then target these potential customers and expand the reach to additional people who may engage with the brand. For example, new regulations, negative news stories, high-profile data breaches and evolving usage of a vendor may all impact the risks associated with your third parties. Some key risk-changing events

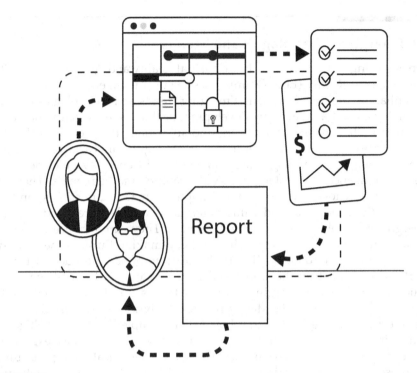

FIGURE 8.5
Monitoring of third-party data.

to monitor include mergers, acquisitions or divestitures, as well as internal process changes. Third-party risk management (TPRM) involves identifying, assessing and controlling risks that occur due to interactions with third parties, including procurement and off-boarding (Figure 8.5). TPRM employs policies and systems to ensure third parties:

- Comply with regulations.
- Avoid unethical practices.

Furthermore, third-party risk management is how companies analyze and control risks involved with vendors and service providers. TPRM is often carried out with the support of frameworks, which provide organizations with roadmaps for building their TPRM programs based on industry-standard best practices. Finally, third-party management solutions are technologies and systems designed to automate the performance of one or more third-party management processes or functions. Such solutions are external-facing and designed to complement internal-facing governance, risk and compliance (GRC) systems and processes.

8.4 Emerging Technologies and Trends

The emerging technology trends are Virtual Reality and Augmented Reality and Extended Reality (ER). VR immerses the user in an environment, while AR enhances their environment. Emerging trends and technologies refer to technologies that are currently developing, or that are expected to be available within the next five to ten years, and are usually reserved for technologies that are creating, or are expected to create, significant social or economic effects. Emerging technologies are characterized by curiosity, quick development, intelligence, noticeable effect, vulnerability and vagueness. They are technologies whose development and application areas are still expanding fast, and their technical and value potential is largely unrealized, though emerging technologies offer several benefits. They can enhance economic growth and efficiency by improving decision-making through the analysis of large amounts of data, leading to the creation of new products, services, markets and industries that boost consumer demand and generate new revenue streams. The top emerging technology trends are AI, augmented reality (AR), virtual reality (VR), big data, advanced analytics, blockchain, cleantech, the Internet of Things (IoT) and robotics. For example, Artificial Intelligence is the simulation of human intelligence processes by machines, especially computer systems. Furthermore, if a trend is a historical change up until the present, then an emerging issue is a possible new technology, a potential public policy issue or a new concept or idea that, while perhaps fringe thinking today, could mature and develop into a critical mainstream issue in the future or become a major trend in its own.

After analyzing more than 150 emerging technologies, PwC categorized AI as one of its Essential Eight technologies. In a cybersecurity risk assessment, risk likelihood is the probability that a given threat is capable of exploiting a given vulnerability that should be determined based on the discoverability, exploitability and reproducibility of threats and vulnerabilities, rather than historical occurrences. Broadly speaking, there are five types of cybersecurity assessments: baseline cybersecurity assessments, penetration testing, red team testing, vulnerability assessments and IT audits. Security assessment is the process of evaluating and analyzing the security measures and protocols in place to protect a system or organization from potential threats and vulnerabilities (Figure 8.6). Threat assessment refers to the process of evaluating and analyzing potential risks and vulnerabilities to an organization's digital assets, networks and systems. A cybersecurity risk assessment is the process of identifying, analyzing and evaluating risk. It helps to ensure that the chosen cybersecurity controls are appropriate to the risks your organization faces. Without a risk assessment to inform your cybersecurity choices, you could waste time, effort and resources. The most common types of cybersecurity assessment include checklist-based evaluation, compliance checking, vulnerability identification and analysis, penetration testing, simulation or

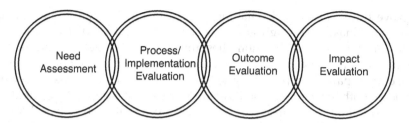

FIGURE 8.6
Regular assessment.

emulation-based testing, formal analysis and reviews. Security assessments are essential tools for businesses of all sizes. They provide an important way to identify and address any vulnerabilities in networks, systems and applications, to protect the business from potential cyber threats. IoT security assessments validate virtually any connected device against a broad range of attacks, known and unknown, so that critical devices can be secured before leaving the development environment. An IT assessment typically includes evaluating hardware, software, network infrastructure, data security measures, backup and disaster recovery systems, IT policies and procedures, as well as assessing the organization's goals, needs and challenges. It is a method used to evaluate students' cognitive ability and performance primarily by accessing personalized education, examination materials and feedback anytime and anywhere, all of which are said to make it more efficient than the traditional assessment. IoT testing, or Internet of Things testing, is the process of verifying the functionality, UX, security, stability and performance of an IoT device. This process involves testing both the hardware and the software components of the product and is therefore unique from the point of view of testing challenges. The goal of an IT assessment is to optimize IT systems to decrease costs, reduce risk and improve governance and security. AI-based assessments are designed to help identify the best candidate based on objective performance criteria. Ideally, AI in assessment is used to prevent human bias from having an undue impact on hiring decisions. The use of AI in assessment isn't a new trend. AI-powered educational assessment tools provide numerous benefits, including improving the accuracy and efficiency of assessments, generating personalized feedback for students and enabling teachers to adapt their teaching strategies to meet the unique needs of each student. AI assessment tools use machine learning to evaluate a candidate's experience and qualifications as they relate to the job description. Intelligence tests measure people's cognitive functioning, including but not limited to verbal, mathematical and visuospatial reasoning, memory, attention and language comprehension and production. AI enhances business risk management by swiftly analyzing complex data to predict and identify potential risks. It ensures companies can preemptively address threats, improving decision-making and resource allocation. AI-powered testing frameworks improve the accuracy and reliability of test results by minimizing human errors and biases. Through advanced analytics and predictive modeling, AI testing tools can detect anomalies, uncover hidden defects and identify risk areas with greater precision. Since impact assessment refers to a specific type of transparency report designed to help stakeholders assess the societal impact to both harms and benefits of an AI system, it is generally created and reviewed before a system is put into use. Implement process-based assessments that break larger assignments into stages such as proposal, outline, draft and final submission, and evaluate each stage. This approach allows instructors to monitor progress and understand students' thought processes, making it harder for students to completely rely on AI. The research and development of a blockchain assessment framework enables the assessment of the technical suitability, high-level design, adoption approach, economic feasibility and business value potential of a blockchain solution with a particular organization for a specific process. Blockchain uses the three principles of cryptography, decentralization and consensus to create a highly secure underlying software system that is nearly impossible to tamper with. There is no single point of failure, and a single user cannot change the transaction records. Blockchain analytics offers access to reliable data without the overhead of operating nodes or developing and maintaining an indexer. We can now query the full history of blocks, transactions, logs and call traces for Ethereum Virtual Machine-compatible blockchains. Big data is a dataset term that describes the large volume of data for structured, semi-structured and unstructured types that have the potential to be mined for information. Every time a user opens email, uses a mobile app, tags on social media, walks into a store, makes an online purchase, talks to a customer service representative or asks a virtual assistant, those technologies collect and process that data for the organization. The key distinctions lie in the sheer volume, variety, and speed they handle. Traditional data deals with structured information in manageable amounts, like a monthly expense report. Conversely, big data takes on the challenge of vast and unstructured data sources, like social media posts, images and sensor readings. Cloud readiness assessments are an indispensable first step that can provide a solid footing before moving forward with plans. A cloud readiness assessment lets you examine your applications and data to determine whether they can be moved to the cloud with minimal impact on operational continuity to determine how ready the organization is to adopt cloud technology and to identify the optimal cloud strategy tailored to its unique needs. At its core, a cloud readiness assessment is about asking the right questions and analyzing the existing setup with a critical eye. A cloud security assessment evaluates the cloud infrastructure for vulnerabilities, configuration weaknesses and potential threats. It analyzes cloud service provider account or subscription configurations and reviews the possible threats from the internet and within the cloud infrastructure itself. Conducting a comprehensive cloud assessment is a critical step in the cloud strategy and readiness process. This assessment evaluates an organization's readiness to migrate to the cloud and identifies potential roadblocks to ensure a seamless cloud experience.

AI is transforming all industries. One of the simplest ways to identify emerging technologies is to follow the trends in your industry and beyond. You can use various sources, such as blogs, podcasts, newsletters, social media, conferences and reports to keep up with the latest developments and insights. Artificial Intelligence is perhaps the largest force in emerging technologies as its applications span across many areas including security, robotics, clouding computing, the Internet of Things (IoT), cognitive automation and finance—to name but a few. The advantages of new technology include increased efficiency, improved communication and enhanced convenience. However, it may lead to job displacement and privacy concerns. After all, emerging technologies have the potential to greatly impact our future society. These technologies can enhance economic growth and efficiency by improving decision-making and creating new products, services, markets and industries, which will boost consumer demand and generate new revenue streams. Consequently, emerging technologies, such as industrial robots, artificial intelligence and machine learning are advancing at a rapid pace. These developments can improve the speed, quality and cost of goods and services, but they also displace large numbers of workers. Furthermore, with the advancements in machine learning and artificial intelligence, robots will be able to learn and adapt to new situations, making them more efficient and effective. In addition to robotics, virtual and augmented reality are also expected to become more integrated into our daily lives in the next decade. However, emerging technologies can also amplify and expand complex social, legal and ethical issues. Due to the simultaneous evolution of these emerging technologies in multiple settings, it is nearly impossible to anticipate and address their impacts on individuals, groups or society as a whole. Meanwhile, emerging technologies such as artificial intelligence, blockchain, cloud computing and big data can offer tremendous opportunities for businesses to innovate, optimize and differentiate. However, they also pose significant risks, such as security breaches, ethical dilemmas, regulatory uncertainties and skill gaps. Hence, if a trend is a historical change up until the present, then an emerging issue is a possible new technology, a potential public policy issue or a new concept or idea that, while perhaps fringe thinking today, could mature and develop into a critical mainstream issue in the future or become a major trend on its own. Historically, the biggest risks faced by foreign investors were in developing countries with immature or volatile political systems. The chief concern was "expropriation risk," the possibility that host governments would seize foreign-owned assets. Emerging things can be brand-new but aren't necessarily: they could just be beginning to develop. Chatbots provide a new and effective form of communication between the brand and consumer and are emerging in all business sectors and catering to various types of services. Furthermore, emerging technologies used in light industries, like AI, IoT and 3D printing, are transforming consumer experiences and manufacturing processes. Trend forecasting, connected clothing and smart homes, rapid prototyping and immersive experiences are major use cases in this sector. As a result, emerging technologies play a vital role in the modernization of industries. New technologies help in transforming enterprises into a digital world. This technology is mainly helpful in manufacturing, energy and mobility markets.

9

Innovations in Cybersecurity

Exploring

9.1 Blockchain, AI and IoT Solutions

Artificial intelligence and blockchain technologies are widely used in the Internet of Things (IoT). IoT for collecting and presenting data, blockchain to provide the infrastructure to define operational rules and AI optimization processes and rules are all possible connections between these technologies. The Internet of Things (IoT) enables devices across the internet to send data to private blockchain networks to create tamper-resistant records of shared transactions. IBM Blockchain® enables business partners to share and access IoT data, but without the need for central control and management. Smart medical devices can be powered by AI to make potentially lifesaving decisions through biometric data. Ethereum Blockchain can make the use of smart contracts very popular owing to its efficiency. The data from the IoT devices can be made to trigger some tasks. By providing access to large volumes of data from within and outside of the organization, blockchain helps AI scale to provide more actionable insights, manage data usage and model sharing and create a trustworthy and transparent data economy. Blockchain is a distributed ledger technology that combines with IoT to make machine-to-machine transactions possible. It uses a set of transactions that are recorded in a database, verified by multiple sources and entered in a common ledger distributed across every node.

Blockchain technology is an advanced database mechanism that allows transparent information sharing within a business network. A blockchain database stores data in blocks that are linked together in a chain. The benefits of blockchain technology in IoT are:

- Enhanced security.
- Data integrity and immutability.
- Decentralization.
- Transparent and auditable transactions.

DOI: 10.1201/9781003604679-9

FIGURE 9.1
Blockchain technology.

- Automated smart contracts.
- Data monetization and ownership.
- Interoperability.
- Reduced costs and improved efficiency.

AI involves analyzing and interpreting data, making informed decisions and predicting outcomes (Figure 9.1). In contrast, blockchain technology revolves around a decentralized ledger that securely stores and verifies data. While AI and blockchain are distinct domains, there are some areas where these two technologies are used together: blockchain is a decentralized, secure ledger system that records transactions, while AI refers to machines mimicking human intelligence. Both technologies prioritize data, with AI analyzing it for insights and blockchain ensuring data integrity and transparency. Hence, the convergence of blockchain and AI has the potential to transform healthcare in powerful ways while maintaining patient privacy.

Energy Optimization: AI algorithms can optimize energy consumption, and blockchain can ensure transparent and secure energy trading in a decentralized grid. Blockchain is a technology designed to create secure and tamper-resistant digital ledgers. It focuses on decentralization and trust. AI aims to create intelligent systems capable of learning, reasoning and decision-making. It focuses on simulating human-like intelligence. As AI systems extract vast amounts of data, blockchains can ensure that the data is transparent, auditable and that there is some provenance to it. Blockchains provide a record of who accesses the data and for what purpose. This data can then be used to extract some meaningful insights.

Blockchain can secure identity and access management for IoT devices, ensuring only authorized devices and users can access and interact with the network, which adds an extra layer of security in IoT ecosystems. The future of IoT is promising, with advancements in edge computing, 5G connectivity, AI integration, blockchain security, industry-specific solutions, sustainability,

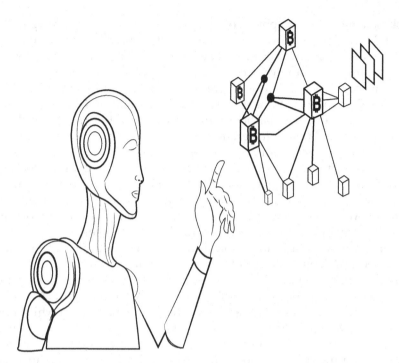

FIGURE 9.2
Intelligent system.

enhanced data analytics and expanded interoperability. Benefits of benefits of IoT and blockchain convergence are:

- Security.
- Privacy.
- No centralized data warehouse required.
- Smart contracts.
- Industry management.
- Supply chain management.

A blockchain is a decentralized, distributed and public digital ledger that is used to record transactions across many computers so that the record cannot be altered retroactively without the alteration of all subsequent blocks and the consensus of the network (Figure 9.2). Furthermore, blockchain facilitates multistep transactions that require verification and traceability. It can ensure secure transactions, lower compliance expenses and accelerate data transfer processing. Blockchain technology can aid in contract administration and product auditing.

Blockchain has so many applications in every sector that you can imagine, such as healthcare, finance, government, identity, etc. And that's not including the most popular application of blockchain, which is Bitcoin. To keep users safe, better security must be developed, maintained and become the standard for IoT and connected devices. This is where blockchain comes into play. Blockchain can track data collected by sensors and block cybercriminals' ability to duplicate that data with other malicious forms of data. As IoT devices typically have limited computing power, integrating blockchain technology may require significant energy resources and may not be practical for low-power devices.

Regulatory Frameworks – Another challenge of integrating blockchain with IoT is the lack of regulatory frameworks. After all, blockchain does not replace AI, because blockchain is not the same as artificial intelligence, although AI can be used in blockchain. In the general context, blockchain provides security while AI provides artificial intelligence to any device, service, or technique. For example, blockchain can be used to create a tamper-proof, decentralized database of all supply chain transactions, and AI can be used to analyze the data in real-time, providing insights into the supply chain that were previously impossible to obtain. Additionally, the AI could be used to analyze market trends and make recommendations on which trades to execute. Overall, the use of AI and smart contracts has the potential to significantly streamline and automate various processes, improving efficiency and reducing the risk of errors and disputes. AI and blockchain are changing businesses in such a way that small businesses have access to improved quality control, traceability and transparency. Moreover, AI has harnessed the abundance and authenticity of data available via blockchain to predict demand, improve inventory management and identify potential disruptions. The most developed use case for AI in crypto is through decentralizing GPU computing power. Both AI and crypto require significant processing power: AI for its data processing and machine learning tasks, and crypto for mining and transaction verification. Both AI and blockchain are decentralized and distributed, meaning that they rely on a network of nodes or computers to function, rather than a central authority. Overall, blockchain technology has a very promising future. In the years to come, we may anticipate seeing even more groundbreaking and novel uses for blockchain as technology advances. Many businesses might be completely changed by blockchain, which would also make the world more transparent and safer. Blockchain is a distributed ledger technology that combines with IoT to make machine-to-machine transactions possible. It uses a set of transactions that are recorded in a database, verified by multiple sources and entered in a common ledger distributed across every node. Moreover, the integration of blockchain with IoT not only bolsters security but also enables enhanced connectivity between devices. With its ability to establish trust among parties without relying on intermediaries, blockchain facilitates seamless peer-to-peer transactions between IoT devices. AI is crucial for IoT because it enhances IoT's capabilities by enabling data analysis, predictive insights, automation and intelligent decision-making. AI processes the vast amount of data generated by IoT devices, making IoT systems smarter, more efficient and capable of proactive actions. Now the benefits of AI and blockchain can bring new value to business processes that span multiple parties—removing friction, adding speed and increasing efficiency. For example, AI models embedded in smart contracts that are executed on a blockchain can take the following actions: Recommend expired products to recall.

9.2 Blockchain for Data Protection

In most blockchains or distributed ledger technologies (DLT), the data is structured into blocks, and each block contains a transaction or bundle of transactions. Each new block connects to all the blocks before it in a cryptographic chain in a way that nearly impossible to tamper with. Blockchain data storage and security represent a revolutionary paradigm shift in the way information is stored, accessed and protected. Blockchain technology supports privacy in multiple ways. As a distributed ledger, a blockchain network has multiple nodes, each containing its public address and private keys, ensuring only the private key holder has access to the information in the nodes. As a blockchain has a distributed ledger, this means that data are stored on multiple nodes in a network. This makes it impossible for attackers to manipulate information by simply hacking a system. The process makes unauthorized changes difficult, hence ensuring confidentiality.

Blockchain data is stored on a decentralized public ledger. The data on the ledger is stored in chunks called blocks, which are chained together using cryptography. Every block has a unique cryptographic hash as an identifier, along with the previous block in the blockchain. Blockchain can improve data storage by encrypting the files and distributing them across the decentralized network, making it harder for hackers to access the data. There is no central entity controlling access to files or possessing the keys needed to decrypt the files. Blockchains manage a large-scale record of transactions and additional data wrapped in several layers of data security. As a result, these systems are generally regarded as safe and secure. The benefits of blockchain privacy are that it can significantly change how to view critical information. By creating a record that can't be altered and is encrypted end-to-end, the blockchain helps prevent fraud and unauthorized activity. Blockchain uses cryptography to secure data on the network. Each transaction on the blockchain is encrypted, and only authorized parties can access the information using their private keys. This ensures that sensitive information is kept confidential and can only be accessed by those with the appropriate permissions. This property makes it immutable, which means that once something has been entered in a blockchain it cannot be tampered with. If a hacker tries

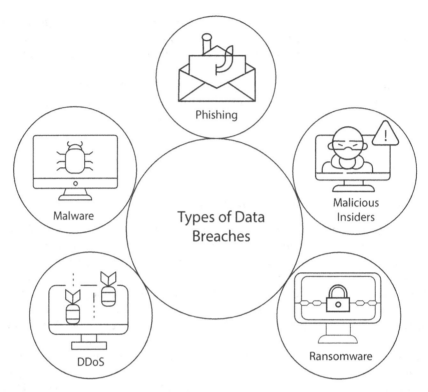

FIGURE 9.3
Types of data breaches.

to tamper with a block, the hash of the block changes, which changes the hash of the subsequent blocks. Consequently, there is a lot of hype behind blockchain; however, there are also many false claims. One in particular is that since blockchain can be used to verify a system of records, traditional databases are no longer needed (Figure 9.3). This is very misleading because blockchain and databases are different types of record systems. Furthermore, a unique and fundamental characteristic of blockchain is its immutability. Once a block of data has been added to the blockchain, it is virtually impossible to alter or delete. This feature is due to the cryptographic hashes linking the blocks together. However, blockchain offers decentralization, immutability and reduced intermediaries, while traditional databases provide consistency, reliability and better scalability for large-scale applications.

As a result, blockchain technology and big data have seen a lot of growth because businesses generate ample data. At this crucial point, blockchain technology emerges as a reliable, cost-effective and decentralized ledger to keep anonymous data generated daily. The system stores the information of transactions that have taken place but doesn't store any personal information or sensitive data. A second way you can learn how to store data on a

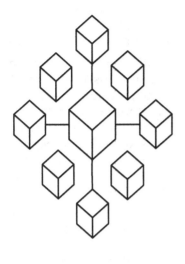 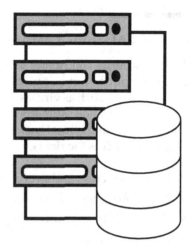

Blockchain   Traditional Databases

FIGURE 9.4
Blockchain vs. traditional databases.

blockchain is by looking at what type of file formats are used. The most efficient way to store the information is by generating the cryptographic hash of
the document and storing that on the blockchain with the timestamp. Hash
values are much smaller than their corresponding documents and save a
huge amount of space and cost. Blockchain also makes it possible for users to
store their passwords without having to trust a centralized third party. This
eliminates the risk of someone maliciously gaining access to data (Figure 9.4).
After all, blockchain is seen as secure for gigantic measures of money due to
its decentralized and cryptographic nature. The development's straightfor-
wardness, perpetual nature and understanding parts add to an incredible
and change-safe system, diminishing the risk of blackmail or unapproved
access. Meanwhile, each newly created block makes it more secure. An
existing blockchain, therefore, cannot be hacked in the traditional sense of
"being hacked," where malicious code is introduced into the chain or someone "hacks" into the network with brute force and begins making changes
or asserting control. Consequently, hybrid blockchain lets organizations set
up a private, permission-based system alongside a public permission-less
system, allowing them to control who can access specific data stored in the
blockchain, and what data will be opened up publicly. Finally, consensus on
data accuracy is required from all network members, and all validated transactions are immutable because they are recorded permanently. No one, not
even a system administrator, can delete a transaction.

9.3 AI and Machine Learning in Cybersecurity

AI in cybersecurity contributes to detecting and classifying malware. Machine learning algorithms can be trained to recognize the characteristics of different types of malware, such as viruses, worms and trojans. Improving business goals through AI automation skills is one interesting career path. On the other hand, if cyber challenges and ethical hacking skills lead towards an adventurous career, then cybersecurity is the right choice. Some examples of AI in cybersecurity are:

- Threat detection and prevention.
- Automated incident response.
- Vulnerability scanning and patch management.
- Threat hunting.
- Malware analysis and reverse engineering.
- Penetration testing and ethical hacking.
- Risk assessment.
- Data loss prevention.

Cybersecurity is one of AI's core applications against a backdrop of a fast-evolving threat landscape. Over the next year, AI will transform cyberthreat detection and risk assessment. Keeping a human in the loop will be essential to responsible AI-powered cybersecurity.

By acting as a force multiplier for seasoned cyber professionals, AI's functions across the cyber lifecycle include monitoring vast swaths of data to detect nuanced adversarial attacks, quantifying the risks associated with known vulnerabilities and powering decision making with data during threat hunts (Figure 9.5). Hence, AI can monitor, analyze, detect and respond to cyber threats in real time. As AI algorithms analyze massive amounts of data to detect patterns that are indicative of a cyberthreat, it can also scan the entire network for weaknesses to prevent common kinds of cyber-attacks. Furthermore, AI-based cybersecurity systems provide improved accuracy and efficiency compared to traditional security solutions. For example, AI can scan multiple devices for potential vulnerabilities in a fraction of the time it would take human operators to do the same task. Hence, it is essential to use AI in cybersecurity for managing network vulnerabilities, given the daily threats companies face. It analyzes existing security measures to identify weak points, enabling businesses to focus on critical security tasks. In terms of a learning curve, it is much easier to step into the field of cybersecurity than it is AI. This is because cybersecurity has various diverging paths, has softer learning prerequisites and requires less effort. AI is a useful part of a cybersecurity toolkit, but it's not an

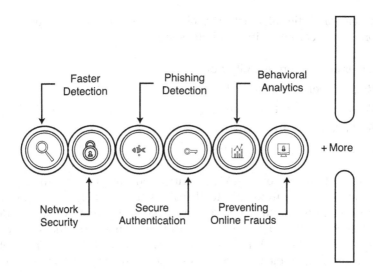

FIGURE 9.5
AI and machine learning in cybersecurity.

all-inclusive solution. While AI can automate and enhance various cyber-security processes, artificial intelligence can only augment, not replace, human expertise in the fast-evolving threat landscape. Consequently, the security professionals will protect businesses from attacks—building the infrastructure to detect and stop threats and test networks for potential vulnerabilities. AI professionals are at the forefront of data analysis. They build tools and models to analyze large datasets to provide insights and perform tasks. As a result, machine learning (ML) is a specific branch of artificial intelligence (AI). ML has a limited scope and focus compared to AI. AI includes several strategies and technologies that are outside the scope of machine learning.

9.4 IoT Security Challenges and Solutions

Some common security challenges for IoT devices include:

Weak Authentication: IoT devices are notorious for their use of weak and default passwords. Several large botnets, such as Mirai, infected many devices simply by logging in using default and hardcoded passwords, even though IoT security (internet of things security) is the technology segment focused on safeguarding connected devices and networks in IoT. IoT involves adding internet connectivity to a system of interrelated computing devices, mechanical and digital machines, objects, animals and people. Effective solutions to IoT connectivity challenges are:

- Diversifying connectivity options.
- Regular network health checks.
- Power sources management.
- Scalable cloud infrastructure.
- Enhanced security protocols.

IoT devices often rely on weak authentication and authorization practices, which makes them vulnerable to threats. For example, many devices use default passwords, making it easier for hackers to gain access to IoT devices and the networks they use for communication, so the main challenge of IoT is security and privacy. As IoT devices are more connected to the internet, they become more vulnerable to cyber-attacks. Ensuring data privacy and security is a major challenge for IoT companies. IoT security is also affected by the cost, changes throughout its evolution and scope of the safety measures taken. All three are major considerations. IoT security is important due to the susceptibility of IoT devices and the growing use of IoT hardware. Many IoT devices remain unencrypted and can act as a gateway for hackers, where one compromised device could grant someone access to its entire connected network.

IoT security refers to the approaches, strategies and technologies used to prevent these devices from being hacked. Robust IoT security encompasses all parts of protection, such as component hardening, monitoring, firmware upkeep, access control, threat response and vulnerability repair. In today's rapidly evolving IoT landscape, businesses are eager to harness the potential of connected technologies, but they face several key challenges (Figure 9.6). One of the major hurdles is the IoT skills gap, where companies struggle to find talent that's well-versed in the complexities of IoT development. IoT security is not traditional cybersecurity, but a fusion of cybersecurity with other engineering disciplines. It addresses much more than mere data, servers, network infrastructure and information security. One of the greatest threats to IoT security is the lack of encryption on regular transmissions. Many IoT devices don't encrypt the data they send, which means if someone penetrates the network, they can intercept credentials and other important information transmitted to and from the device. Additionally, manufacturers occasionally include hardcoded passwords in their systems that users cannot change. These weak passwords place the IoT devices at high risk, as attackers can simply log into these devices with these easily guessed passwords or simple brute-force attacks. Cybersecurity encompasses all of the technology and operations employed to safeguard devices and their respective platforms and networks from cyberattacks or hacking. Similarly, IoT is the term used to refer to all the objects and devices that are interconnected by one source

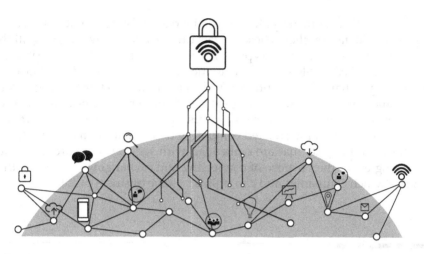

FIGURE 9.6
IoT security.

of the internet. Furthermore, IoT devices can collect vast amounts of data on workplace conditions, allowing the analysis of safety trends and the identification of potential hazards. This information can be used to develop strategies to enhance workplace safety and prevent accidents. Wherever security measures, such as surveillance systems, access control and trained security personnel, provide a sense of safety and personal protection, they act as a deterrent against criminal activities, making individuals feel more secure in public spaces, workplaces and residential areas. The enhanced security and privacy of IoT and video surveillance can also help to increase the users' and the systems' security and privacy. To prevent unwanted access to data and devices, video surveillance and IoT can employ access control, authentication and encryption techniques. Consequently, the IoT service vulnerabilities can present new entry points to other devices connected to home networks, such as laptops and computers. If these devices are used to work from home or as part of a bring-your-own-device (BYOD) policy, hackers may also be able to gain access to corporate networks. However, sensors play an important role in creating solutions using IoT. Sensors detect external information, replacing it with a signal that humans and machines can distinguish. There are challenges, too. Data security is a major concern in the IoT space, and startups need to ensure that their products are safe from cyber threats. Additionally, the lack of standardization in IoT technology can make it difficult for startups to integrate their solutions with existing systems. Internet of Things (IoT) devices are computerized Internet-connected objects, such as networked security cameras, smart refrigerators and Wi-Fi-capable automobiles. IoT security is the process of securing these devices and ensuring they do not introduce threats into a network. Most network traffic originating from IoT devices is unencrypted, which increases the possibility of security threats and data breaches. These threats can be avoided by ensuring all the devices are secured and encrypted. Future trends in IoT, like security surveillance marked by blockchain integration, AI-driven threat detection, edge computing, enhanced encryption, multi-factor authentication and regulatory compliance, are poised to create a safer and more reliable environment for the deployment of interconnected devices. As a result, IoT solutions are the integrated system of interrelated computing devices, mechanical and digital machines and objects that are embedded with sensors, software and other technologies for the purpose of connecting and exchanging data with other devices which companies and can utilize to solve business problems.

9.5 Case Studies and Practical Examples

9.5.1 Elevating a Housing Association's Security Posture with Managed XDR for Microsoft

The Challenge: As one of the largest housing associations in the UK, Southern Housing was concerned about being targeted due to a sharp increase in cyberattacks on its industry. The organization also needed to broaden its defenses in response to the shift to remote and hybrid working. By delivering enhanced threat visibility and complete response, the responder-managed detection and response has enabled Southern Housing to maximize its technology investment while also assuring the security of its IT infrastructure and assets.

9.5.2 The Impact

9.5.2.1 Comprehensive Threat Visibility

Taking telemetry from Microsoft Defender 365's product suite to identify, close and neutralize threats, working with Southern Housing's security team for remediation activity for full coverage and deep insight of its environments. Because Kroll Responder is highly user-friendly, Southern Housing's security team can easily identify key details and ensure that nothing is missed when they do need to carry out further investigation.

9.5.2.2 Security Telemetry Unified Across the Microsoft Security Stack

Southern Housing benefits from faster and more effective identification and shutdown of threats through the capacity to unify security telemetry across the Microsoft Defender stack, along with any third-party EDR, network, cloud and Software as a Service (SaaS) providers across the Microsoft ecosystem.

9.5.2.3 Actionable Security Intelligence

Southern Housing now has peace of mind that the risk of security incidents is minimized and managed through the Responder's custom rules in combination with the centralized network, directly derived from frontline IR investigations. This is further enhanced through regular updates with insights drawn from Kroll's wide range of cyber functions and status as the world's No. 1 provider.

9.5.2.4 Expert Security Guidance

The 24×7 support provided through the Responder frees up Southern Housing's security team to focus on educating internal teams. They also have direct access to global team of SOC analysts, giving them the advantage of personalized, expert support. With help always at hand to provide assurance or to confirm whether an alert signifies a genuine threat or a false-positive, Southern Housing benefits from the peace of mind of having a second set of eyes on its entire Microsoft estate.

9.6 Building Cyber-Resilience Amid Azure Migration

The Challenge: With ransomware increasing and a complex, business-critical cloud migration on the horizon, BSM, one of the world's largest shipping companies, was seeking a solution to monitor its environment for potential threats, both now and in the future. Working with that gives the company greater visibility across its global network of offices and ships to better detect and respond to threats. Teams within them help BSM to navigate and deploy appropriate security controls and processes, which include those related to its Microsoft Security strategy, continuously monitoring systems using that Responder-managed detection and response, and ultimately building a more effective and resilient IT infrastructure while meeting compliance obligations.

9.6.1 The Impact

9.6.1.1 Enhanced Threat Visibility

The shipping company now has enhanced threat visibility across its global network of offices, ships and public cloud environments. It uses the latest security intelligence to detect current and emerging threats and constantly tunes the underlying technology, included as part of that Responder, to reduce false positives.

9.6.1.2 Swift Incident Response

It provides the outcomes and actionable mitigation guidance needed to be able to quickly respond to incidents and significantly reduce the possibility of an attack. Incident information is shared securely via Redscan's threat management platform. Then the SOC teams thoroughly analyze and investigate every security alert received and, if the alert is deemed to be a genuine incident, use the Redscan threat management platform to notify the client, relay the incident's priority level and supply the information needed to assist in remediation.

9.6.1.3 Improved Vulnerability Management

For added security, it offers a broader portfolio of solutions and support: for example, penetration testing engagements, conducted by the team of CREST-certified experts and designed to identify and help address hidden vulnerabilities across the company's infrastructure.

9.6.1.4 Professional Service

The level of service offered continually gives BSM peace of mind. From the monthly service reports to personal engagement from both the technical and managerial teams, it is this collaboration that allows the tripart relationship between BSM, Microsoft and Kroll to work so seamlessly and be aligned for the future evolution of the security market and threat landscape.

9.7 Seamless Response to Ransomware and a Cyber-Resilience Upgrade

The Challenge: The company was in the process of rolling out its EDR solution with the aim of understanding the typical volume of around-the-clock alerts it received, before it decided further enhancements were needed to its cybersecurity strategy. As part of this, the company was reviewing how its team managed alerts; while it had a 24/7 response team, it was not dedicated specifically to security operations. The company was looking for a way to cost-effectively scale up the team and its capabilities using a specialist in threat response.

As the rollout of the EDR solution was taking place, along with the conversation about handling out-of-hours alerts, the company was hit by a ransomware attack. In response, the company appointed Kroll as its digital forensics and incident response firm.

9.7.1 The Impact

9.7.1.1 Seamless Incident Response Support

The rapid incident response delivered by a global network of certified security and digital forensics experts enabled the ransomware attack to be managed and mitigated effectively and quickly, allowing the company to get back up and running as soon as possible.

9.7.1.2 Comprehensive Attack Analysis and Recovery

The digital forensics experts analyzed the ransomware attack to quickly and safely uncover critical information to aid recovery. This enabled the company to gain a comprehensive understanding of the vulnerabilities that may have led to the attack, highlighting critical areas for improvement and enhancing its resilience against future attacks.

9.7.1.3 Actionable Threat Intelligence

The company benefits from the intelligence gains through responding to 3,000+ incidents every year, with insights drawn from multiple events, clients, sources and experts. Continually updated threat intelligence passed back into triage helps to inform the company's in-house team and enhances detection capabilities.

9.7.1.4 360-Degree Threat Visibility

The company now has continual and comprehensive visibility of threats. The Responder's tech- agnostic approach allows this intelligence to fuel detection and build a more resilient, integrated organization, from Security Information and Event Management (SIEM) and EDR to vulnerability scanning and behavioral monitoring.

9.7.1.5 Maximize In-House Security Team

The Responder's 24/7 monitoring capabilities have maximized the benefits of the company's in-house security team, allowing it to focus its attention on systems that are particularly complex or difficult to manage. The company security team now benefits from a world-class team of threat analysts, seeing real-time frontline threat intelligence from incident response cases while alleviating the requirement of recruiting and maintaining the skillset of an in-house, out-of-hours security team. Alongside this, the regular service reviews provided as part of the Responder MDR service enable the company to stay continually up-to-date with the profile and level of its risk. That provides a vital checkpoint while also removing the administrative burden from the company.

9.7.1.6 Enhanced Cyber-Resilience

The company gained valuable insights through incident response and post-incident investigation. This, combined with the ongoing monitoring and threat intelligence provided by the Responder, means that the company is much better placed to defend against ransomware attacks and other cyber threats in the future, ultimately creating a stronger foundation for the company's ongoing cybersecurity strategy.

10

Charting the Course

Successes, Failures and Insights for Tomorrow's Data Guardians

10.1 Successful Implementations of Data Protection Strategies

Some of the most common types of data security, which organizations should combine to ensure they have the best possible strategy, include encryption, data erasure, data masking and data resiliency. The primary goal of data protection is not just to safeguard sensitive information but to ensure that it remains accessible and reliable, thus preserving trust and compliance in data-centric operations. Data protection strategies typically involve multistep processes that define how security measures are implemented and maintained. The goal is to minimize the footprint of sensitive data and secure business-critical and regulated data.

Data protection is the process of protecting sensitive information from damage, loss or corruption. The amount of data being created and stored has risen at an unprecedented rate, making data protection increasingly important. In general, cybersecurity focuses on protecting an organization's systems and networks against cyber threats, such as ransomware, phishing, etc. Cyber protection brings in an increased focus on data security, combining elements of cybersecurity and data protection. For example, data privacy is ensuring that sensitive data, such as financial information or medical records, is only accessed by authorized personnel. This can be achieved through access control measures, such as usernames and passwords, or biometric authentication. Encrypting data is another example of data privacy. Data encryption is crucial for protecting information both while it is being sent and when it is stored. IoT devices often send sensitive data, and encrypting this data makes sure that even if someone intercepts it, they cannot read it. Utilize encryption methods like AES or DES to secure data transmitted by IoT devices. It is key to implement data protection strategies, including antivirus programs, automated monitoring, data visibility solutions and strong

DOI: 10.1201/9781003604679-10

passwords with multi-factor authentication to safeguard sensitive information. IoT helps to improve workplace safety by providing real-time monitoring and alerts, predictive maintenance, employee tracking, improved
compliance and increased efficiency. Internet of things devices are computerized Internet-connected objects, such as networked security cameras, smart
refrigerators and Wi-Fi-capable automobiles. IoT security is the process of
securing these devices and ensuring they do not introduce threats into a network. After all, IoT security is the technology segment focused on safeguarding connected devices and networks in IoT. IoT involves adding internet
connectivity to a system of interrelated computing devices, mechanical and
digital machines, objects, animals and people. However, IoT security refers
to the approaches, strategies and technologies used to prevent these devices
from being hacked. Robust IoT security encompasses all parts of protection,
such as component hardening, monitoring, firmware upkeep, access control,
threat response and vulnerability repair. Furthermore, security in IoT
involves implementing various strategies, technologies and best practices to
protect IoT devices, networks and data from unauthorized access and potential threats. This includes strong authentication, encryption, secure firmware
updates and robust network security, among other measures. IoT security is
important due to the susceptibility of IoT devices and the growing use of IoT
hardware. Many IoT devices remain unencrypted and can act as a gateway
for hackers, where one compromised device could grant someone access to
its entire connected network. Adobe has introduced an app to help creators
protect their work against AI copycats. Content Authenticity is a free web
app that lets creators receive attribution for their work with Content
Credentials, which the tech company calls a nutritional label for digital materials. Encryption ensures that data, both at rest and in transit, is unreadable
to unauthorized individuals. Applying strong encryption algorithms and
managing encryption keys securely can safeguard sensitive data from inter-
ception and unauthorized access. AI data analytics is designed to support,
automate and simplify each stage of the data analysis journey. AI tools can
help with data collection of ingesting from multiple sources and preparation
for cleaning and organizing for analysis data. AI can use machine learning
and natural language processing techniques to detect and correct data errors,
such as typos, duplicates, missing values, outliers and inconsistencies. For
example, AI can identify and standardize different formats of dates, names,
addresses and currencies across different data sources. Data is the lifeblood
of artificial intelligence, providing the information needed to train AI models
and make accurate predictions. Without data, AI systems cannot learn or
make informed decisions. For example, training a facial recognition model
requires a large dataset of images to accurately identify faces. Artificial intelligence (AI) is increasingly utilized in various security aspects to enhance
threat detection, incident response and overall cybersecurity. Some key ways
AI is used in security include Advanced Threat Detection and Anomaly
Detection that identifies unusual patterns indicating potential threats. AI

safety, a combination of operational practices, philosophies and mechanisms, aims to ensure that any developed AI systems and models operate in the manner originally envisioned by the developers without resulting in any unintended consequences or harm. Privacy by Design in an AI approach involves minimizing data collection to what's strictly necessary, securing data and giving users control over their information. By adopting this framework, AI developers can build systems that inherently protect personal information, addressing privacy concerns proactively. When ensuring the development of safe and transparent AI systems, it is crucial to invest in research focused on mitigating potential risks. These risks can include biases in data or models, the potential for malicious use, and unintended consequences that may arise from the use of AI systems. AI primarily monitors and analyzes behavior patterns. By using these patterns to create a baseline, AI can detect unusual behaviors and restrict unauthorized system access. AI can also help to prioritize risk, instantly detecting the possibility of malware and intrusions before they begin. After all, AI's capability to monitor environments in real-time, predict potential hazards, personalize safety training and even take over hazardous tasks marks a significant leap forward in protecting employees. Furthermore, every transaction on the blockchain is secured with cryptographic principles, ensuring data integrity and authentication. Public key infrastructure (PKI) grants users a public key to receive assets and a private key to safeguard them. To implement a blockchain solution security model, administrators must develop a risk model that can address all business, governance, technology and process risks. Next, they must evaluate the threats to the blockchain solution and create a threat model. A zero-knowledge proof, known as a ZKP, is a cryptographic method by which one party, the prover, can prove to another party, the verifier, that a given statement is true, without conveying any information apart from the fact that the statement is indeed true. Blockchains are used as a digital ledger to store transactional information. The data is stored as signed blocks which link to each other, creating a chain of immutable interconnected data entries. To sign a new block, a node needs to find an SHA-256 signature that matches specific criteria. When one of the participants needs to add a new data item to the blockchain, they first symmetrically encrypt it using the secret key. Then the transaction with the encrypted data is submitted to the blockchain. Blockchain uses cryptographic algorithms to secure data, eliminating the need for a central authority. Hence, it provides inherent data integrity and confidentiality since data stored on the blockchain is encrypted using cryptographic algorithms, making it immutable to anyone without the corresponding decryption keys. Encryption ensures that sensitive information remains secure even if unauthorized access to the blockchain occurs. Blockchain security is a complete risk management system for blockchain networks, incorporating assurance services, cybersecurity frameworks and best practices to mitigate the risks of fraud and cyber-attacks. However, the hyperledger method is used to store data on private blockchains. Hyperledger includes organizations, and the data stored for each organization can be combined at the time of reading the stored data. Astra DB is the DBaaS of choice for blockchain applications because of its unique combination of low latency at global scale, massive data on any cloud and server-less, pay-as-you-go pricing. After all, data privacy defines who has access to data, while data protection provides tools and policies to actually restrict access to the data. Compliance regulations help ensure that users' privacy requests are carried out by companies, and companies are responsible for taking measures to protect private user data. This comprehensive understanding and application of the Four Vs of big data, Volume, Velocity, Variety and Veracity, are fundamental for crafting an effective big data strategy. Furthermore, a Big Data strategy is a comprehensive plan that outlines how an organization will manage, store, analyze and use large volumes of data to achieve its goals. All of this involves converting complex datasets, such as transaction records, social media interactions, sensor data and website logs, into valuable information.

To implement data protection by design and default by those steps could range from changing the personal data that is processed so that it is only that information which is necessary for the particular purpose, implementing technical measures to give notices or obtain consent (as required) or putting in place access controls or techniques such as pseudonymization. The three main data protection policies are:

- Data security—protecting data from malicious or accidental damage.
- Data availability—quickly restoring data in the event of damage or loss.
- Access control—ensuring that data is accessible to those who actually need it, and not to anyone else.

Data protection safeguards information from loss through backup and recovery (Figure 10.1). Data security refers specifically to measures taken to protect the integrity of the data itself against manipulation and malware. It provides a defense from internal and external threats. Data privacy refers to controlling access to the data. As a result, the most effective way to protect against data loss is to back up data regularly. Saving multiple copies of your data should be a regular part of your business's routine. There are many ways to do this, such as external hard drives. Storing data on an external hard drive is a basic, inexpensive and easy way to back up data. Consequently, use strong passwords, implement firewalls, update software regularly, monitor network traffic and conduct regular security audits. However, the best practice is a combination of encryption, access control, regular backups and employee training. Having a solid data protection strategy in place will help businesses standardize data security and prevent unauthorized access to private information. Data protection is not only required by law; it is essential to safely conduct business of all kinds. There are nine key elements in data

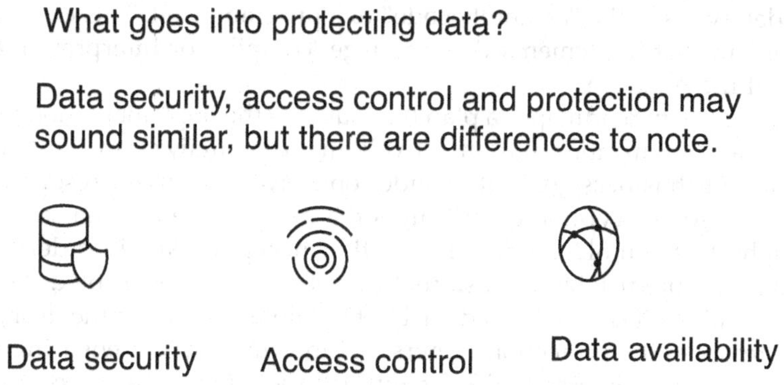

What goes into protecting data?

Data security, access control and protection may
sound similar, but there are differences to note.

Data security   Access control   Data availability

FIGURE 10.1
Successful implementations of data protection strategies.

protection policy, some of which are the introduction and scope, definitions, GDPR principles, roles and responsibilities of those handling data, data breach notification procedures.

It is important to have good data protection practices from fraud and cybercrimes. Applying strong data protection measures and safeguards not only protects individuals' or customers' personal data but also your organization's data, therefore avoiding considerable problems, which could damage your reputation or your organization's confidential information. Data protection by default requires users to ensure that it only processes the data that is necessary to achieve a specific purpose. It links to the fundamental data protection principles of data minimization and purpose limitation. The seven principles of the GDPR are: Lawfulness, fairness and transparency; purpose limitation; data minimization; accuracy; storage limitation; integrity and confidentiality; and accountability. These principles are found right at the outset of the GDPR, and they inform and permeate all other provisions of that legislation. Employee data protection is the act of ensuring that applicable privacy and data protection laws are followed regarding employee information. This means, of course, ensuring the data is stored securely, but also informing employees when the organization shares all or any of their data with a third party. If the company handles personal data, it's important to understand and comply with the principles of the GDPR.

The three states of data are data at rest, data in motion and data in use. Data can change states quickly and frequently, or it may remain in a single state for the entire life cycle of a computer. One of the core functions of a DLP strategy and solution is to prevent exposing sensitive data to unauthorized parties. Organizations today are faced with the challenge of selecting the best security solutions. This includes implementing a SIEM and IDS/IPS to protect their corporate data. However, the implementation of the datatype is in the c compiler itself—in the code/logic of the compiler, hence it can't "see" datatypes in the "assembly code" of a program itself. This exists in the mechanism that implements the language (compiler or interpreter), not in the resulting program.

A data strategy roadmap is a plan that outlines the implementation process for how an organization will effectively manage, analyze and utilize data to achieve its business goals. It includes objectives, necessary resources and a timeline. An encryption algorithm is the method used to transform data into ciphertext. An algorithm will use the encryption key in order to alter the data in a predictable way, so that even though the encrypted data will appear random, it can be turned back into plaintext by using the decryption key. It refers to the protection of personal information and ensuring that it is not misused or accessed without authorization. One example of data privacy is ensuring that sensitive data, such as financial information or medical records, is only accessed by authorized personnel. As a result, data protection and privacy are typically applied to personal health information (PHI) and personally identifiable information (PII). It plays a vital role in business operations, development and finances.

10.2 Lessons Learned from Data Breaches and Incidents

An example would be an employee using a co-worker's computer and reading files without having the proper authorization permissions. The access is unintentional, and no information is shared. However, because it was viewed by an unauthorized person, the data is considered breached. Even T-Mobile experienced its ninth data breach in five years, with 37 million customer records stolen in November 2022. The attack utilized an AI-equipped API to gain unauthorized access, exposing sensitive client information such as full names, contact numbers and PINs. Although hacking attacks are frequently cited as the leading cause of data breaches, it's often the vulnerability of compromised or weak passwords or personal data that opportunistic hackers exploit. The concepts behind blockchain technology make it nearly impossible to hack into a blockchain. However, weaknesses outside of the blockchain create opportunities for thieves. Hackers can gain access to cryptocurrency owners' cryptocurrency wallets, exchange accounts or the exchanges themselves. Data aggregator National Public Data (NPD) has finally confirmed a breach that has exposed personal identity records belonging to potentially hundreds of millions of consumers across the US, UK and Canada.

However, learning cybersecurity helps in planning and implementing security strategies to reduce risk and enhance the protection of information, assets and systems. It also helps in communicating effectively, verbally and in writing with corporate management on cybersecurity-related issues. In addition, in today's digital world, one cannot ignore cybersecurity. One single

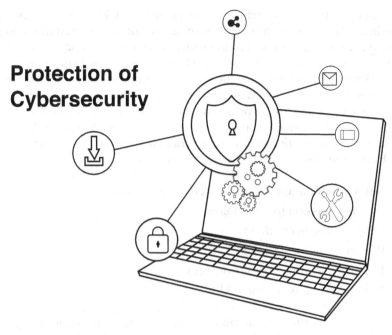

Protection of Cybersecurity

FIGURE 10.2
Lessons learned from data breaches and incidents.

security breach can lead to exposing the personal information of millions of people (Figure 10.2). These breaches have a strong financial impact on the companies and also loss of customer trust. Meanwhile, the biggest impact of security breaches is that depending on the type of data involved, the consequences can include destruction or corruption of databases, the leaking of confidential information, the theft of intellectual property and regulatory requirements to notify and possibly compensate those affected. Data leaks can reveal everything from social security numbers to banking information. Once a criminal has these details, they can engage in all types of fraud under your name. Theft of your identity can ruin your credit, pin you with legal issues, and it is difficult to fight back against. Implement a lockout for multiple failed login attempts. If credentials have been compromised, reset passwords as soon as possible. Discourage users from reusing the same password across critical services such as banking and social media sites, or sharing passwords for a critical service with a non-critical service. The impact of a data breach on individuals can be devastating. It can cause financial loss, damage credit scores and lead to emotional distress. You may have to spend hours or even days sorting through your finances, canceling credit cards and changing passwords to ensure that your personal information is secure. Data breaches can create permanent damage to a company's reputation. Criminal breaches can result in a monetary fine, which is imposed by the courts as a penalty in criminal proceedings. Criminal breaches by individuals may also result in jail time. Sometimes data breaches affect the economy in such a way that they compromise legally protected information identifying individuals accessing various services, from financial and healthcare to social services. Data breaches also directly impact the economy as their cost continues to rise over 20% year-on-year, amounting to 4–6% of the global gross domestic product.

The three basic security concepts important to information on the internet are confidentiality, integrity and availability. Concepts relating to the people who use that information are authentication, authorization and nonrepudiation. Hence the best way to learn cybersecurity is:

- Build a foundation with an introductory course.
- Evaluate passion for technology.
- Learn a little every day.
- Become an ethical hacker.
- Practice in simulated environments.
- Mix it up with workplace skills.

Every element of the information security program must be designed to implement one or more of the three main principles. In today's world, cybersecurity is critical because of security threats and cyberattacks. For data protection, many companies develop software. This software protects the data. Cybersecurity is important because it not only helps to secure information but also our systems from virus attacks. Furthermore, organizations are finding themselves under the pressure of being forced to react quickly to the rapidly increasing number of cybersecurity threats. Since attackers have been using an attack life cycle, organizations have also been forced to come up with a vulnerability management life cycle. Meanwhile, a robust data security management and strategy process enables an organization to protect its information against cyberattacks. It also helps them minimize the risk of human error and insider threats, which continue to be the cause of many data breaches. The purpose of a lessons-learned session is to share and use the knowledge gathered from a security incident to facilitate positive outcomes and prevent the recurrence of negative outcomes.

Furthermore, software skills are necessary to learn how to work with cloud security environments, computer systems and different operating systems. And you should also know how to use software packages, such as office suites and anti-virus programs. You need to know the different types of data, how they are classified and when to call in a forensic expert. Finally, an information breach can have highly damaging effects on businesses, not only through financial losses but also the reputation damage it causes to customers, clients, and employees.

10.3 Interviews with Industry Experts and Practitioners

10.3.1 An Interview with Ahmet Aksoy—University of Central Missouri

Dr. Ahmet Aksoy is an assistant professor in the Department of Computer Science and Cybersecurity at the University of Central Missouri. As the Director of the cutting-edge NetML (Network Machine Learning) Lab, Dr. Aksoy leads groundbreaking research in the field of network traffic fingerprinting. His research focuses on incident classification, software and device identification through the innovative application of machine learning algorithms.

10.3.1.1 Summary of the Interview

In this interview, Dr. Ahmet Aksoy, an assistant professor at the University of Central Missouri, talked about cybersecurity education opportunities at UCM. Dr. Aksoy discusses his journey into cybersecurity and machine learning, as well as his research focus on network traffic fingerprinting and incident classification.

He explains how machine learning can be used for automated anomaly detection and behavioral analysis in cybersecurity. Dr. Aksoy also provides advice for students interested in pursuing a career in cybersecurity, emphasizing the importance of programming skills, networking fundamentals and cybersecurity certifications. He highlights promising career paths in cybersecurity, such as incident responder, penetration tester, security consultant and security architect.

Dr. Aksoy also discusses the ethical considerations in cybersecurity education and the future of his research, which includes host profiling and user fingerprinting.

10.3.2 An Interview with Faisal Kaleem—Metro University

Dr. Faisal Kaleem is a professor in the Department of Computer Science and Cybersecurity at Metro State in Saint Paul, Minnesota. He is also the director of cybersecurity programs at Metro State and the Executive Director of MN Cyber.

10.3.2.1 Summary of the Interview

In this interview with Dr. Faisal Kaleem, a professor in the Department of Computer Science and Cybersecurity at Metro State and the director of cybersecurity programs there, discusses cybersecurity education opportunities and strategies for career advancement in the field.

Dr. Kaleem shares his own journey into cybersecurity, emphasizing the importance of curiosity and passion for technology. He also highlights the core subjects and skills that students should focus on, including computer science fundamentals, programming languages, computer networking, operating systems, cybersecurity principles, cryptography, web vulnerabilities and security tools and technologies. Dr. Kaleem emphasizes the importance of continuous learning and recommends professional certifications such as CompTIA Security+, Certified Ethical Hacker, Certified Information Security Manager, Certified Information Security Systems Auditor, CISSP, Offensive Security Certified Professional and certifications offered by SANS.

He also discusses the impact of emerging technologies like AI and machine learning on cybersecurity, both from a threat perspective and a defender perspective. Dr. Kaleem advises early-career professionals to pursue further education, stay updated with industry trends, join professional organizations, attend training workshops and conferences, seek mentorship and guidance, contribute to open-source projects and embrace continuous improvement and lifelong learning in their cybersecurity careers.

10.3.3 An Interview with Kathleen Hyde—Champlain College

Kathleen Hyde is the director of Champlain College's online cybersecurity programs. She also teaches Champlain's War Games Capstone in the graduate program. Kathleen holds an MBA and a Master of Science in Computer Information Systems and is currently working on her doctoral dissertation.

10.3.3.1 A Summary of the Interview

In this interview on the Cybersecurity Guide podcast, host Steve Bowcut interviews Kathleen Hyde, the Director of Champlain College's online cybersecurity programs. Hyde discusses her background in cybersecurity and how she became interested in the field.

She also provides an overview of the cybersecurity programs offered at Champlain College, including undergraduate and graduate programs, academic certificates and specializations. Hyde emphasizes the importance of developing power skills, such as problem-solving and communication, in addition to technical knowledge and skills. She also mentions the opportunities for internships and research projects available to students.

Hyde recommends staying informed about industry news, regulations and global perspectives on cybersecurity. Looking into the future, she predicts that artificial intelligence and quantum computing will play a significant role in shaping the cybersecurity landscape. Hyde advises students to adopt a mindset of lifelong learning and to avoid complacency in the ever-changing field of cybersecurity.

10.4 Future Outlook of Cybersecurity

The future of cybersecurity is closely connected to quantum computing, because quantum computers could change how we protect and use data. Right now, most of the ways we keep information safe in cybersecurity rely on the fact that some math problems are really hard for regular computers to solve.

The future of cybersecurity in banking will be shaped by the evolution of advanced technologies and increasingly stringent regulatory frameworks. As cyberattacks become more sophisticated, banks will turn to innovations such as AI-driven security systems, blockchain and quantum computing to enhance their defenses. Cybersecurity in banking involves various measures and protocols designed to protect financial institutions and their customers from cyber threats. The main goal of cybersecurity in the banking sector is to ensure the integrity, confidentiality and availability of sensitive financial data. Cyberattacks affect banks in many ways. In addition to the monetary loss that results from hackers stealing money from banks, they incur additional costs in implementing cybersecurity to protect assets. Furthermore, cyberattacks decrease the trust that customers have in institutions. The National Institute of Standards and Technology's (NIST) cybersecurity framework is the gold standard for cybersecurity. Cyberbanking means such services are offered by the bank over different electronic delivery channels including but not limited to the internet, mobile and fixed-line telephone networks and such other channels as announced by the bank as available. Global spending on security and risk management is set to increase 14.3% in 2024, more than IT spending as a whole at 8%. And Fortune Business Insights expect the cybersecurity market to reach $424.97 billion by 2030, nearly 2.5 times its 2023 valuation.

Cybersecurity in healthcare involves the protecting of electronic information and assets from unauthorized access, use and disclosure. There are three goals of cybersecurity, which are protecting the confidentiality, integrity and availability of information, also known as the CIA triad. Hospitals and other healthcare organizations are highly susceptible to cyberattacks, including ransomware and data breaches, due to their vast collections of sensitive and valuable patient information, limited resources, legacy software and need to interface with specialized medical technologies. Though theft of patient and employee data. Extortion by encrypting data or disabling systems. Hacktivists smearing an organization's reputation through online vandalism and by disclosing company records. Employee negligence, such as losing a laptop or forgetting to encrypt an email. The HCISPP is ideal for information security professionals charged with guarding protected health information (PHI), including those in positions such as compliance officer, information security manager and privacy officer. The Health Insurance Portability and Accountability Act (HIPAA) is a cybersecurity framework that requires healthcare organizations to implement controls for securing and protecting the privacy of electronic health information. After all, hacking and IT incidents have consistently been the most common type of breach, and the number of healthcare data hacking cases increases each year mainly due to ransomware attacks. However, healthcare cybersecurity protects healthcare organizations from external threats, like ransomware or hackers seeking to steal sensitive personal information to sell on the dark web. Hence, the process for conducting risk and vulnerability assessments can be broken down into the following steps. Asset classification by identifying all the assets that hold risk within the IT ecosystem, organizations can begin to assign value, criticality, and operational importance to these assets. Common cybersecurity threats for educational institutions include ransomware attacks, phishing, credential theft, insider sabotage and web application attacks. These cyber threats pose significant risks to students' personal and academic lives. For instance, cyberbullying has become a prevalent issue, causing severe emotional distress and even leading to tragic consequences such as self-harm or suicide. Educational institutions and schools hold a treasure trove of information from personal data to intellectual property, making cybersecurity a crucial concern. Cybersecurity in this sector is vital not only for protecting sensitive information but also for ensuring the continuity of educational services. Cybersecurity awareness empowers students in their future academic and working journey, preparing them for possible cyber challenges. Regular practice, real-world simulations and constant reminders around the campus will help learners become more aware of different types of cyber-attacks and ways to reply to them. Cybercriminals may monitor the activities of students, instructors and others at a school or institution, and even use this information to abuse or threaten students or teachers. Cybercriminals may steal or damage educational data over an unsecured network. The most common cybersecurity threats leveraged against the education sector include malware attacks and ransomware attacks.

To satisfy that demand, the International Information System Security Certification Consortium predicts the worldwide cybersecurity workforce needs to grow by 89%. The market for professionals with advanced cybersecurity skills has expanded at a remarkable rate—from $3.5 billion in 2004 to $150 billion in 2021. The scope of cybersecurity in 2025 seems bright and promising as our reliance on digital technology increases. Since the domain to secure networks, devices, data stored in the cloud and other crucial information is cybersecurity only, the demand for cybersecurity will be high. In the next five to ten years, prevention and preparedness will be more vital than ever. If 2023 taught the cybersecurity industry anything, it's that proactively planning for a cybersecurity incident or data breach is critical. One of the positive trends that could emerge by 2030 is the improvement and advancement of cybersecurity technologies, practices and awareness. After all, AI is a useful part of a cybersecurity toolkit, but it's not an all-inclusive solution. While AI can automate and enhance various cybersecurity processes, artificial intelligence can only augment, not replace, human expertise in the fast-evolving threat landscape. A combination of AI and human expertise will be necessary to ensure a secure and resilient digital world. Because the industry is in such high demand, the opportunity for professionals to build skills and grow in a variety of areas and levels is high as well. For example, the job outlook for cybersecurity is predicted to grow 32 percent over the next decade. The average across all other industries is just five percent. Data science is involved with the interpretation of data to provide actionable insights to businesses and cybersecurity guards to all systems, devices and networks for protection from potential threats.

11

Into the Future

Predictions, Innovations, and Proactive Strategies in Data Protection

11.1 Predictions for the Future of Digital Data Protection

Consumers will more actively manage their data. Consumers are less likely to 'trust the process' and instead will leverage their expanded rights to manage their data in privacy legislation (e.g. granting the right to erasure, data portability). Legislative protection is rapidly expanding. In 2024, the National Cybersecurity Alliance (NCA), a key organizer of Data Privacy Day in the United States, decided on the theme—Take Control of Your Data. Data Privacy Day in 2024 was celebrated from January 21st to 27th. In the UK, the Data Protection Act of 2018 controls how your personal information is used by organizations, businesses or the government. The act is the UK's implementation of the General Data Protection Regulation (GDPR). Data analytics is projected to continue to be in high demand due to the growing emphasis on data-based decision-making in companies and organizations, coupled with the continued advancement of big data and artificial intelligence technologies. In an era of multi-cloud computing, data owners must keep up with both the pace of data growth and the proliferation of regulations that govern it—especially regulations protecting the privacy of sensitive data and personally identifiable information (PII). The objective of Data Privacy Day is to create a more privacy-aware society, reduce the risks of data breaches and identity theft and promote a global digital ecosystem where privacy is respected and protected. After all, the purpose of Data Privacy Day is to raise awareness and promote privacy and data protection best practices. It is currently observed in the United States, Canada, Qatar, Nigeria, Israel and 47 European countries. According to the National Cybersecurity Alliance, engaging in online activities generates a vast amount of data, and individuals possess the authority to assert control over their own data. Furthermore, the GDPR has a chapter on the rights of data subjects (individuals), which includes the right of access, the right to rectification, the right to erasure, the

 DOI: 10.1201/9781003604679-11

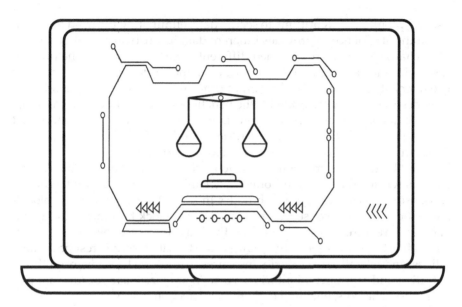

FIGURE 11.1
Predictions for the future of digital data protection.

right to restrict processing, the right to data portability, the right to object and the right not to be subject to a decision based solely on automation.

Although both data protection and privacy are important and the two often come together, these terms do not represent the same thing (Figure 11.1). Although it uses cybersecurity frameworks, assurance services and best practices to reduce risks against attacks and fraud. Blockchain technology produces a structure of data with inherent security qualities. It's based on principles of cryptography, decentralization and consensus, which ensure trust in transactions. Blockchain injects transparency and traceability into supply chain networks. Through smart contracts, stakeholders can automate and secure transactions, significantly reducing the risk of counterfeit products, fraud and unauthorized access to sensitive information within the supply chain. Blocks are files stored by a blockchain, where transaction data are permanently recorded. A block records some or all of the most recent transactions not yet validated by the network. Once the data are validated, the block is closed. Since blockchains are used as a digital ledger to store transactional information, the data is stored as signed blocks that link to each other, creating a chain of immutable interconnected data entries. To sign a new block, a node needs to find an SHA-256 signature that matches specific criteria. Blockchain supports data privacy through its decentralized and transparent nature. It uses cryptographic techniques to secure data, ensuring immutability, anonymity and control over personal information, reducing reliance on centralized entities and providing enhanced privacy protection. Blockchain uses cryptographic algorithms to secure data, eliminating the need for a central authority. Hence, it provides inherent data integrity and confidentiality. Blockchain networks are designed differently in that the logs of the transactions with the data set are used to formulate the world state of the data. The use of cryptographic authentication of time-stamped blocks of transactions provides the whole network with the benefit of certainty of the entire transactional history. By creating a record that can't be altered and is encrypted end-to-end, the blockchain helps prevent fraud and unauthorized activity. That can address privacy issues on the blockchain by anonymizing personal data and by using permissions to prevent access. A block of data on a blockchain is written on an append-only model and gets locked by undergoing a consensus process, during which nodes in the network confirm the block's authenticity. Once a consensus is achieved, the block becomes locked, and altering it requires the agreement of the majority of the network's nodes. After all, AI improves security by enhancing threat detection, response capabilities, and overall cybersecurity measures in areas such as advanced threat detection and real-time monitoring. Then AI analyzes data for unusual patterns and behaviors, enabling early threat detection.

Homomorphic Encryption: This form of encryption allows AI algorithms to process encrypted data, ensuring data privacy even during analysis. AI primarily monitors and analyzes behavior patterns. Using these patterns to create a baseline, AI can detect unusual behaviors and restrict unauthorized access to systems. AI can also help to prioritize risk and instantly detect the possibility of malware and intrusions before they begin. AI security is the process of using AI to enhance an organization's security posture. With AI systems, organizations can automate threat detection, prevention and remediation to better combat cyberattacks and data breaches. Cloud data security protects data that is stored at rest or moving in and out of the cloud from security threats, unauthorized access, theft and corruption. It relies on physical security, technology tools, access management and controls and organizational policies. Though cloud data loss prevention or Cloud DLP is now part of sensitive data protection, a family of services designed to help you discover, classify and protect your most sensitive data. Sensitive data protection includes data discovery, inspection, de-identification, data risk analysis and the DLP API. Cloud providers offer features such as encryption at rest and in transit, identity and access management or IAM and anomaly detection. Secure configuration of storage services, monitoring for unauthorized access and implementing backup and disaster recovery plans are essential aspects. Once data is transferred to Google Cloud for storage, Google Cloud applies encryption at rest by default at the storage level using AES256. A number of different teams within an organization could be responsible for cloud security, such as the network team, security team, apps team, compliance team or the infrastructure team. Although cloud data breaches while data stored in the cloud is encrypted are rare, there are still ways that attackers can bypass encryption through brute force attacks or by stealing login credentials. However, this is not always an issue, as some companies encrypt all their data as soon as it's uploaded to the cloud.

Data privacy is focused on defining who has access to data, while data protection focuses on applying those restrictions. However, data protection safeguards information from loss through backup and recovery. Data security refers specifically to measures taken to protect the integrity of the data itself against manipulation and malware. It provides defense from internal and external threats. Data privacy refers to controlling access to the data. The Data Protection Act in Scotland is that the General Data Protection Regulation (GDPR) regulates and protects the processing of personal data about individuals by using the law to protect our data and the way it is used by third parties and by recognizing that personal data is a valuable asset which must be safeguarded and actively managed. The General Data Protection Regulation (GDPR) is a new, Europe-wide law that replaces the Data Protection Act 1998 in the UK. It is part of the wider package of reform to the data protection landscape that includes the Data Protection Act 2018 (DPA 2018).

Predictive analytics uses historical data to predict future events. Typically, historical data is used to build a mathematical model that captures important trends. That predictive model is then used on current data to predict what will happen next, or to suggest actions to take for optimal outcomes. Since the popularity of IoT devices will generate a massive amount of data, these devices collect and store data in real-time. Not only that, but they also analyze that data and provide insights and personalized recommendations. IoT devices will play a significant role in shaping the future of big data. The GDPR aims to clarify the legal basis for processing personal data, ensuring that organizations have a legitimate reason to collect, use and share individuals' information. Wherever the privacy laws aim to give individuals control over their data back, they empower them to know how their data is being used, by whom and why. After all, internet privacy is important because it gives you control over your identity and personal information. Without that control, anyone with the intention and means can manipulate your identity to serve their goals, whether it is selling you a more expensive vacation or stealing your savings. As a result, Data Protection Day commemorates the Jan. 28, 1981, signing of Convention108, the first legally binding international treaty dealing with privacy and data protection—reported by the National Cyber Security Alliance. Furthermore, data security is an essential foundation for effective data privacy. It ensures that personal data is protected from unauthorized access and misuse, allowing organizations to comply with regulations, maintain trust and uphold ethical data handling practices. Finally, data security involves protecting data from unauthorized access and preventing data from being corrupted or stolen. Data integrity is typically a benefit of data security but only refers to data accuracy and validity rather than data protection.

11.2 Areas of Innovation and Research in Cybersecurity

One element of cybersecurity innovation is using biometric and password-less authentication systems to strengthen online security. Biometric authentication technology allows user authentication with unique biological information, such as fingerprints, facial recognition and iris scans. As though the trending topics for research in cybersecurity field such as an exciting mobile cybersecurity research paper topic for detecting mobile phone hacking. Assessing the threat of using portable devices to access banking services. Cybersecurity and mobile applications. The vulnerabilities in wireless mobile data exchange. Cybersecurity is made up of three main areas: physical, technical and human. In order to exercise the best cybersecurity practice, all three elements need to be considered. The domains of cybersecurities include:

- Security and risk management.
- Asset security.
- Security engineering.
- Communications and network security.
- Identity and access management.
- Security assessment and testing.
- Security operations.
- Software development security.

The five great functions of cybersecurity are: Identify, Protect, Detect, Respond and Recover. NIST defines the framework core on its official website as a set of cybersecurity activities, desired outcomes and applicable informative references common across critical infrastructure sectors. After all, cybersecurity can be broken down into three main pillars: people, processes and technology. Understanding these important components can allow you to use them as a road map to deliver quality IT service and cybersecurity protection. There are two ways one can think about these pillars. Consequently, the AI-powered solutions can sift through vast amounts of data to identify abnormal behavior and detect malicious activity, such as a new zero-day attack. AI can also automate many security processes, such as patch management, making staying on top of your cybersecurity needs easier. However, the NICE Framework comprises seven categories, including: securely provision, operate and maintain, oversee and govern, protect and defend, etc. By automating threat detection and response by AI, cybersecurity systems can not only identify but also respond to threats automatically. AI-powered systems automate threat detection processes, providing real-time monitoring and rapid response times so that unsupervised machine learning in cybersecurity can identify hidden patterns or data groupings without human intervention. The algorithm scans through data sets, looking for patterns used to group information into subsets. Unsupervised machine learning is most commonly used for deep learning, though the research and innovation can generate advances that help cybersecurity keep up with the evolving cyber risks. This helps create a trusted and resilient digital environment. Now the term "security researcher" is often used interchangeably with "ethical hacker," "white hat hacker" or "hacker." These terms describe a cybersecurity professional who uses their skills to identify and address security vulnerabilities in computer systems, networks or applications. Cybersecurity research can shed light on issues with data protection—and the tools and processes that provide it. After all, cybersecurity is the practice of protecting computer systems and networks from unauthorized access or attack. Individuals, businesses and governments must invest in cybersecurity to protect their data and assets from criminals. Consequently, cybersecurity is a process that's designed to protect networks and devices from external threats. Businesses typically employ cybersecurity professionals to protect their confidential information, maintain employee productivity and enhance customer confidence in products and services. Furthermore, when working as a security researcher, the most common skills needed to perform job and for career success are Programming Languages, Scripting Languages, Python, Javascript and PHP. However, a security researcher can spend his time: Analyzing data and searching for patterns; Analyzing malware to know how it works and what it targets; Performing source code review to find potential vulnerabilities. AI can also automate many security processes, such as patch management, making staying on top of your cybersecurity needs easier. Finally, for example, one could focus on a particular type of cyber-attack or a specific cybersecurity technology, then conduct thorough research by reading relevant literature, reviewing case studies, and analyzing real-world examples.

11.3 Recommendations for Staying Ahead of Evolving Threats

- Creating data backups and encrypting sensitive information.
- Updating all security systems and software.
- Conducting regular employee cybersecurity training.
- Using strong and complex passwords.

The best way to remain aware about the latest cybersecurity attacks and their mitigation is to install security patches and updates.

AI has the potential to generate malware that could evade detection by current security filters, but only if it is trained on quality exploited data. There is a realistic possibility that highly capable states have repositories of malware that are large enough to effectively train an AI model for this purpose. AI can analyze past attacks and threat intelligence feeds to identify patterns and predict potential future attacks. This enables security teams to take preventative measures and bolster defenses before an attack even occurs. This proactive approach significantly enhances the overall security posture. The first solution to overcome the threat of AI is through education and training. Governments, educational institutions and companies need to work together to develop training programs that provide new skills to workers who may be impacted by automation. The future of AI is likely to be shaped by a combination of technological advancements, increased investment and changing societal attitudes towards the technology. One of the most significant areas of growth for AI is expected to be in the field of machine learning. The bottom line is that AI is not a threat to humanity; instead, it holds immense potential to shape a remarkable and promising future. When used responsibly, AI becomes a driving force for progress, propelling us towards a world full of endless opportunities.

However, the proliferating data centers that house AI servers produce electronic waste. They are large consumers of water, which is becoming scarce in many places. They rely on critical minerals and rare elements, which are often mined unsustainably. This kind of self-trained, or 'buttered', AI has recently been shown in limited research settings to provide more helpful summaries, write better code and exhibit enhanced commonsense reasoning. AI can cause improper sharing of data when it infers additional sensitive information from raw data. Increased availability and AI make sensitive information more accessible to a wider audience than intended. Intrusion and AI technologies invade personal space or solitude, often through surveillance measures. After all, to stop further use and development of this technology would require a global treaty—an enormous hurdle to overcome. Shapers of the agreement would have to identify the key technological elements that make AI possible and ban research and development in those areas, anywhere and everywhere in the world. Among the most prevalent threats in IoT security are device hijacking, data breaches and distributed denial-of-service (DDoS) attacks. Device hijacking occurs when attackers gain unauthorized access to IoT devices, allowing them to manipulate device functionality, steal data or launch further attacks. However, another current trend in IoT development is so-called edge computing. This strategy involves processing data close to the location where it was collected and will be used. In other words, this approach makes it possible not to send data to a cloud platform to be processed and transferred back. One of the greatest threats to IoT security is the lack of encryption on regular transmissions, which means if someone penetrates the network, they can intercept credentials and other important information transmitted to and from the device.

An Emerging Threat in the context of computer science refers to a new or evolving source of attack or risk that has the potential to harm a system or organization. It includes threats such as novel attack techniques, sophisticated attackers or vulnerabilities that are not yet widely known or addressed. These attacks are designed and executed to perform malicious acts against a system, which has the effect of disrupting services for authorized users, also compromising privacy and the integrity of the system. Examples of active attacks include denial of service, distributed denial of service and man in the middle. Threat modeling of a specific device and its use cases is the systematic process of identifying the sensitive assets, threats to those assets and vulnerabilities that make the threats a necessary concern. The aim is to define security requirements that mitigate the threats and in turn protect the assets. IoT has evolved from the convergence of wireless technologies, microelectromechanical systems and micro services. All these advancements have facilitated seamless connectivity and data exchange between devices and the cloud. The future of IoT involves a deeper integration with AI, the widespread adoption of 5G, the use of digital twins for asset management, the growth of edge computing and continued expansion in supply chain applications. Threat analysis is a cybersecurity strategy that aims to assess an organization's security protocols, processes and procedures to identify threats and vulnerabilities and gather knowledge of a potential attack before it happens. Having access to a user's credentials and other sensitive information can result in losses for the user and the blockchain network. Blockchains rely on real-time large data transfers. Hackers can intercept data as it's transferring to internet service providers. Over time, this ability expanded to include other cryptocurrencies and new features like smart contracts, which automatically execute agreements. As blockchain technology matured, it gained attention from businesses and institutions, leading to new applications like decentralized finance (DeFi) and non-fungible tokens (NFTs). One of the primary challenges associated with integrating blockchain into the realm of cybersecurity is its scalability and energy consumption. While blockchain's decentralized nature is one of its strengths, it also contributes to its limitations. You can mitigate threats by following blockchain security best practices. Users should implement robust encryption and Identity and Access Management (IAM) solutions. Secure development practices, multi-signature wallets, fail-safes, regular audits and Zero Trust Security solutions mitigate blockchain security risks. The ability to manage a large number of users at a single time is still a challenge for the blockchain industry. Blockchain technology involves several complex algorithms to process a single transaction. The public nature of blockchains can make sensitive information vulnerable. To counter these privacy challenges, cutting-edge cryptographic techniques like zero-knowledge proofs (ZKPs) and confidential transactions are increasingly employed. One of the primary concerns with big data is the potential for data privacy breaches and security vulnerabilities. Collecting and analyzing large volumes of data increases the risk of unauthorized access, data leaks and cyber-attacks, posing privacy and security risks for individuals and organizations.

Installing updates and security patches on a regular basis is a critical step for mitigating cyber risk. The faster security gaps are closed, the less opportunity there is for cybercriminals to exploit vulnerabilities in unpatched or outdated software. By educating employees on the best practices for cybersecurity, such as using strong passwords, identifying phishing emails and reporting suspicious activity, organizations can reduce their risk of a cyber-attack. Creating security policies and practices is essential for protecting your company from cyber-attacks. This includes establishing rules for password creation, access controls and data sharing. It is also important to develop a data protection plan in case of a data breach. To prevent cyber-attacks by prioritizing cybersecurity, organizations can mitigate the risk of data breaches, financial losses and reputational damage. Whether it's an individual or an organization, understanding the importance of cybersecurity is fundamental to navigating the threat landscape safely and securely. Cybersecurity is one of the most important aspects of the fast-paced growing digital world. The threats of it are hard to deny, so it is crucial to learn how to defend from them and teach others how to do so, too.

Several ways to protect systems from online threats are:

- Keep computers and mobile devices up to date.
- Set strong passwords.
- Watch out for phishing scams.
- Keep personal information personal.
- Secure internet connection.
- Shop safely.
- Read the site's privacy policies.

Furthermore, the importance of cyber safety is the fact that one single security breach can lead to exposing the personal information of millions of people. These breaches have a strong financial impact on the companies as well as loss of customer trust. Hence, cybersecurity is very essential to protect businesses and individuals from spammers and cyber-criminals. You can think of it as a plan that outlines how an organization will protect itself from cyber events. A mature cyber defense strategy should include multiple measures such as vulnerability management, incident response and security awareness training. Consequently, the methods of defense in cybersecurity are:

1 To install and maintain the hardware and software for security infrastructure.
2 Analyzing, identifying, and patching system vulnerabilities within the network.
3 Implementing real-time solutions to diffuse zero-day attacks.

FIGURE 11.2
Recommendations for staying ahead of evolving threats.

Cyber defense refers to the practices, strategies and technologies employed to protect computer systems, networks and data from cyber threats, unauthorized access and attacks (Figure 11.2). It encompasses a range of measures to detect, prevent and respond to cyber threats. As a result, internet security is a broad term that refers to a wide range of tactics that aim to protect activities conducted over the internet.

Implementing internet security measures helps protect users from different online threats like malware, phishing attacks, scams and even unauthorized access by hackers. Furthermore, the goal of cybersecurity is to ensure secure storage, control access and prevent unauthorized processing, transfer or deletion of data. It safeguards the confidentiality, integrity and availability of information. Finally, it can provide clients with the best-in-class security solution to meet the three main objectives of cybersecurity: protect the confidentiality, integrity and availability of sensitive information, systems and data.

Conclusion

In conclusion, *Guardians of Data: A Comprehensive Guide to Digital Data Protection* serves as a beacon of knowledge in the ever-evolving landscape of cybersecurity. Throughout this journey, we have explored the fundamental principles of digital data protection, delving into the intricacies of safeguarding information in an increasingly interconnected world.

We have emphasized the importance of understanding digital data, recognizing its diverse forms and vulnerabilities. From legal and regulatory frameworks to emerging threats and innovative technologies, we have equipped ourselves with the knowledge and tools necessary to defend against cyber adversaries.

As we reflect on the key concepts and strategies discussed, it becomes evident that continuous vigilance is paramount in the realm of data protection. Cyber threats are dynamic and ever-evolving, requiring proactive measures and constant adaptation to stay ahead of the curve. In closing, let us remain steadfast in our commitment to protecting digital assets and upholding the principles of integrity, confidentiality and availability. The journey towards data security is ongoing, but with dedication, resilience and collective effort, we can ensure a safer digital future for generations to come.

DOI: 10.1201/9781003604679-12

Bibliography

Abawajy J. (2014). User preference of cyber security awareness delivery methods. Behavior & Information Technology, 33(3), 237–248.

Adrian M. (2017). Running the risk IT—More perception and less probabilities in uncertain systems. Information & Computer Security, 25(3), 45–59.

Alberts C., Carol W. (2007). Considering operational security risk during system development. IEEE Security & Privacy, 5(1), 30–35.

Alfonsi A., Rabiti C., Mandelli D., Cogliati J. J., Kinoshita R. A. (2013). Raven as a tool for dynamic probabilistic risk assessment: Software overview. International Conference on Mathematics and Computational Methods Applied to Nuclear Science & Engineering, 5(4), 456–467.

Algarni A., Xue Y., Chan T. (2017). An empirical study on the susceptibility to social engineering in social networking sites: The case of Facebook. European Journal of Information Systems, 26(6), 661–687.

Ana F., Gabriele L. (2016). An analysis of social engineering principles in effective phishing. IEEE, 3(5), 33–49.

Andress A. (2003). Surviving security: How to integrate people, process and technology. 2nd ed. Auerbach Publications.

APCERT. (2014). Computer Security Incident Response Teams (CSIRTs) report, 2014.

Appin Security Group. (2017). Information Security Management Practices Report.

Applegate S. D. (2009). A global perspective of social engineering: Hacking the wetware. Information Security Journal: A Global Perspective, 18(1), 40–46.

Ayesha M., Muhammad M. (2013). Security framework for cloud computing environment: A review. Journal of Emerging Trends in Computing and Information Sciences, 3(3), 91–101.

Bedford T., Cooke R. (2015). Probabilistic risk analysis: Foundations and methods. Cambridge University Press.

Bill G., Valerie T. (2016). Building an information security awareness program: Defending against social engineering and technical threats. Elsevier Copyright.

Bob B., Ellen M., Dan G. (2005). Information security is information risk management. Proceedings of the 2001 Workshop on New Security, 4(1), 97–104.

Boltz J. (2015). Informational security risk assessment: Practices of leading organizations. Diane Publishing.

Brill A., Pollit M., Whitcomb C. M. (2013). The evolution of computer forensic best practices: An update on programs and publications. Journal of Digital Forensic Practice, 1(1), 3–11.

Bruce K. (2023). PRIVACY IMPACT ASSESSMENT (PIA). National Institute of Standards and Technology, NIST Baldrige National Quality Program.

Buskirk E. V., Liu V. T. (2006). Digital evidence: Challenging the presumption of reliability. Journal of Digital Forensic Practice, 1(1), 19–26.

Cheung S. K. S. (2014). Information security management for higher education institutions. Intelligent Data Analysis and Its Applications, 1(2), 55–68.

Chivukula R., Lakshmi T. J., Ranganadha Reddy Kandula L., Alla K. (2021). A study of cyber security issues and challenges. IEEE Bombay Section Signature Conference (IBSSC), Gwalior, 1–5.

Choo K. R., Kermani M. M., Azarderakhsh R., Govindarasu M. (2017). Emerging embedded and cyber physical system security challenges and innovations. IEEE Transactions on Dependable and Secure Computing, 14(3), 235–236.

Chowdhury N., Gkioulos V. (2021). Cyber security training for critical infrastructure protection: A literature review. Computer Science Review, 40, 567–580.

Christopher H. (2013). Managing information security risks: The octave approach. Addison- Wesley Longman Publishing.

Christopher H. (2018). Social engineering: The science of human hacking. John Wiley & Sons.

Cojazzi G. (1996). Preliminary requirements for a knowledge engineering approach to expert judgment elicitation in probabilistic safety assessment. International Conference on Probabilistic Safety Assessment and Management, 24(2), 491–498.

Cojazzi G., Fogli D. (2001). Benchmark exercise on expert judgment techniques in PSA level 2. Nuclear Engineering and Design, 1(3), 211–221.

Cojazzi G., Keejam. (2003). Benchmark exercise on expert judgment techniques. Nuclear Engineering and Design, 21(1), 211–221.

Conteh N. Y., Schmick P. (2016). Cybersecurity: Risks, vulnerabilities and countermeasures to prevent social engineering attacks. International Journal of Advanced Computer Research, 23(6), 345–360.

Conway B. A. (2010). Calibrating expert assessments of advanced aerospace technology adoption impact. Dominion University Journal, 3(1), 22–29.

Cooke R. M., Abigail R. (2017). Cross validation for the classical model of structured expert judgment. Reliability Engineering & System Safety, 163(1), 109–120.

Cooke R. M., Goossens L. L. H. J. (2010). TU delft expert judgment data base. Reliability Engineering & System Safety, 93(5), 657–674.

Cooke R. M., Julie C., Ryana T. (2012). Quantifying information security risks using expert judgment elicitation. Computers & Operations Research, 39(4), 774–784.

Creery A., Byres E. J. (2005). Industrial cybersecurity for power system and SCADA networks. Record of Conference Papers Industry Applications Society 52nd Annual Petroleum and Chemical Industry Conference, 303–309.

Cremonini M., Nizovtsev D. (2009). Risks and benefits of signaling information system characteristics to strategic attackers. Journal of Management Information Systems, 26(3), 241–274.

Daniel D., Yuval E. (2016). A model of the information security investment decision-making process. Computers & Security, 63(4), 1–13.

D'Arcy J., Herath T., Shoss M. K. (2014). Understanding employee responses to stressful information security requirements: A coping perspective. Journal of Management Information Systems, 31(2), 285–318.

Donn B. (2013). Toward a new framework for information security. John Wiley & Sons.

Duff A. S. (2007). Social engineering in the information age. An International Journal, 21(1), 67–71.

Dwyer F., Schurr P., Ohior S. (1999). Developing buyer-seller relationship. Journal of Marketing, 51(2), 11–19.

Edward H. (2015). Implementing the ISO/IEC 27001 information security management system standard. The ACM Digital Library, 11(2), 109–120.

Eisenhardt K. M. (1989). Agency theory: An assessment and review, academy of management. The Academy of Management Review, 14(1), 57–61.

Ekelhart A., Fenz S., Neubauer T. (2009a). AURUM: A framework for information security risk management. System Sciences (HICSS). Annual Hawaii International Conference, 4(2), 30–39.

Ekelhart A., Fenz S., Neubauer T. (2009b). Ontology-based decision support for information security risk management. ICONS International Conference, 2(1), 79–87.

Eloff M., Solms S. (2014). Information security management: A hierarchical framework for various approaches. Computers & Security, 19(3), 243–256.

Ericson C. A., II. (2016). Hazard analysis techniques for system safety. John Wiley & Sons.

Eyong K. (2014). Recommendations for information security awareness training for college students. Information Management & Computer Security, 3(2), 33–45.

Fabrigar L. R., Wegener D. T. (2014). Exploratory factor analysis. Oxford University Press.

Fan W., Kevin L. (2017). Social engineering: I-E based model of human weakness for attack and defense investigations. Computer Network and Information Security, 9(1), 1–11.

Feriel D., Selmin N. (2014). A benchmarking framework for methods to design flexible business processes. Software Process: Improvement and Practice, 12(1), 51–63.

Georg D. (2014). ISO/IEC 27000, 27001 and 27002 for information security management. Journal of Information Security, 4(2), 92–100.

Georgiadou A., Mouzakitis S., Askounis D. (2022). Working from home during COVID-19 crisis: A cyber security culture assessment survey. Security Journal, 35, 486–505.

Gerben S., Peter E., Margareta W., Gerard G. (2015). Managing risk and resilience. Academy of Management Journal, 58(4), 305–314.

Gerring J. (2015). Social science methodology: A criterial framework. Cambridge University Press.

Gewald H., Wollemscbcr K., Weitzel T. (2014). The influence of perceived risks on banking managers intention to organizational business process—A study of German banking and finance industry. Journal of Electronic Commerce Research, 7(2), 78–96.

Godbole N. (2017). Information system security, security management, metrics, framework and best practices. John Wiley & Sons, Inc.

Gregory R., Hancock L., Stapleton R. (2018). The Reviewer's guide to quantitative methods.

Gurpreet D., Syed R., Cristiane P. (2016). Interpreting information security culture: An organizational transformation case study. Computers & Security, 56(2), 63–69.

Halliday Badenhorst S., Solms V. (2003). A business approach to effective information technology risk analysis and management. Information Management and Computer Security, 4(1), 19–31.

Harold F., Micki K. (2013). Information security management handbook. Taylor & Francis Group.

Hartini S., Zaiton H. (2011). The application of the digital signature law in securing internet banking: Some preliminary evidence from Malaysia. Procedia Computer Science, 3(1), 248–253.

Hartini S., Zaiton H. (2013). The application of the digital signature law in securing internet banking: Some preliminary evidence from Malaysia. Procedia Computer Science, 3(2), 248–253.

Harwood I. A. (2006). Confidentiality constraints with mergers and acquisitions. Gaining insights through a 'bubble' metaphor. British Journal of Management, 1(7), 347–359.

Hawkins S. M., Yen D. C., Chou D. C. (2000). Disaster recovery planning. A Strategy for data security.

Heidi W., Maumita B. (2016). Countering social engineering through social media: An enterprise security perspective. Journal of Computational Collective Intelligence, 14(2), 54–64.

Heidi W., Maumita B., Rafiqul I. (2014). Social engineering through social media: An investigation on enterprise security. International Conference on Applications and Techniques in Information Security, 5(3), 243–255.

Hichem S., Fateh G., Sidi S., Hassnaa M., Jiajia L., Shuai H. (2020). Cyber security based on artificial intelligence for cyber- physical systems. IEEE Network, 34(3), 6–7.

Hinson G. (2007). The state of IT auditing in 2007. The EDP Audit, Control, and Security Newsletter, 36(1), 13–31.

Hinson G. (2008). Social engineering techniques, risks, and controls. The EDP Audit, Control, and Security Newsletter, 37(4), 32–46.

Hinson G. (2011). Handbook of research on social and organizational liabilities in information security. Taylor & Francis Group.

Hinson G. (2013). Information security management metrics: A definitive guide to effective security monitoring and measurement. The EDP Audit, Control, and Security Newsletter, 43(3), 9–15.

Hinson G., Brotby W. K. (2016). PRAGMATIC security metrics: Applying metametrics to information security. CRC Press, Taylor & Francis Group.

Jacques B., Rossouw V. (2004). A cyclic approach to business continuity planning. Information Management & Computer Security, 12(4), 328–337.

Jeb W., Atif A., Maynard G. (2015). A situation awareness model for information security risk management. Computers & Security, 44(2), 1–15.

Joana A. (2024). Secure Software Development: What are the Key Best Practices for Success? Tech Insights.

Joe F., Christian M., Marko S. (2012). PLS-SEM: Indeed a silver bullet. Journal of Marketing Theory and Practice, 19(2), 139–152.

Joe F., Hair J., Marko S., Lucas H., Volker G. (2015). Partial Least Squares Structural Equation Modeling (PLS-SEM): An emerging tool in business research. European Business Review, 7(2), 79–89.

Joseph F., Jeffrey R., Marko S., Christian M. (2019). When to use and how to report the results of PLS- SEM. European Business Review, 25(3), 456–469.

Joseph F., Tomas M. (2016). A Primer on Partial Least Squares Structural Equation Modeling (PLS- SEM). SAGE Publications.

Ju M., Kim S., Kim T.-N. (2017). A study on digital media security by Hopfield neural network. Advances in Neural Networks, 5(1), 140–153.

Juhani A., Kari J., Jorma K., Ilkka K. (2013). Integrating ISO/IEC 27001 and other managerial discipline standards with processes of management in organizations. 2012 Seventh International Conference (IEEE), 6(2), 73–89.

Justin W., Eggstaff T., Mazzuchi S. (2014). The development of progress plans using a performance- based expert judgment model to assess technical performance and risk. Systems Engineering, 22(6), 471–484.

Kaplan R. (2010). A matter of trust, information security management handbook. 5th ed. CRC Press.

Katharina K., Heidelinde H., Markus H., Edgar W. (2015). Advanced social engineering attacks. Journal of Information Security and Applications, 22(3), 113–122.

Kaur J., Ramkumar K. R. (2022). The recent trends in cyber security: A review. Journal of King Saud University—Computer and Information Sciences, 34(8), 5766–5781.

Kebande V. R., Venter H. S. (2018a). Novel digital forensic readiness technique in the cloud environment. Australian Journal of Forensic Sciences, 50(5), 552–591.

Kebande V. R., Venter H. S. (2018b). On digital forensic readiness in the cloud using a distributed agent-based solution: Issues and challenges. Australian Journal of Forensic Sciences, 50(2), 209–238.

Khan A. W., Zaib S., Khan F., Tarimer I., Seo J. T., Shin J. (2022). Analyzing and evaluating critical cyber security challenges faced by vendor organizations in software development: SLR based approach. IEEE Access, 10, 65044–65054.

Kim E. B. (2013). Information security awareness status of business college: Undergraduate students. Information Security Journal: A Global Perspective, 22(4), 171–179.

Kliem R. (2008). Managing the risks of offshore IT development. The EDP Audit, Control, and Security Newsletter, 32(4), 12–20.

Korchenko O., Vasiliu Y., Gnatyuk S. (2014). Modern quantum technologies of information security against cyber-terrorist attacks. Journal of Aviation, 14(2), 58–69.

Linstone M. (1999). The Delphi method techniques and applications. Addison Wesley.

Logan M. S. (2000). Using agency theory to design successful organizational relationship. International Journal of Logistics Management, 11(2), 21–31.

Louis A. (2010). What's wrong with risk matrices? Wiley Online Library, 28(2), 497–512.

Lund S., Den Braber F., Stolen K., Vraalscn F. (2015). A UML profile for the identification and analysis of security risks during structured brainstorming. STEF Technical Journal, 4(3), 220–234.

Malacaria P. (2007). Assessing security threats of looping constructs. Proc. ACM Symposium on Principles of Programming Language, 3(1), 56–67.

Malacaria P., Chen H. (2008). Lagrange multipliers and maximum information leakage in different observational models. Proceedings of the third ACM SIGPLAN workshop on Programming languages and analysis for security Journal, 5(1), 135–146.

Malaysian Cyber Security. (2018). The Malaysian public and private sector information security risk assessment methodology.

Malhotra N. K. (1996). Marketing research and applied orientation. 4th ed., New York, NY: Prentice Hall.

MAMPU. (2019). The Malaysian public sector information security High-Level Risk Assessment (HiLRA) guide. National Library of Malaysia.

Manes G. W., Downing E. (2010). What security professionals need to know about digital evidence. Information Security Journal: A Global Perspective, 19(3), 124–131.

Mann I. (2018). Hacking the human: Social engineering techniques and security countermeasures. Taylor & Francis Group.

Manske K. (2006). An introduction to social engineering. Information Systems Security, 9(5), 1–7.

Manske K. (2008). An introduction to social engineering. Information Systems Security, 9(5), 1–7.

Maria E., Garcia U., Josefina L., Murillo L. (2017). Application of the Delphi method for the analysis of the factors determining social entrepreneurship. Journal of Business, 9(1), 43–66.

Marian C., Karen R., Stephen M., O'Brien C. (2017). A framework for information security governance and management. IT Professional, 18(2), 22–30.

Markus H., Stewart K., Marcus N. (2009). Towards automating social engineering using social networking sites. International Conference on Computational Science and Engineering, 8(1), 65–77.

Marshall K., Matthew S., Philip K. (2018). Cyber risk management for critical infrastructure: A Risk analysis model and three case studies. Wiley Online Library, 38(2), 226–241.

McMurray I., Brownlow C. (2016). SPSS explained. Taylor & Francis Group.

Menezes A. J., van Oorschot P. C., Vanstone S. A. (1997). Handbook of applied cryptography. CRC Press.

Michael J. (2007). Information management system: The organizational dimension. Oxford University Press.

Mike M. (2024). Privacy Risk Assessments: DPIAs and PIAs. Clarip Inc.

Mohamed G., Sophia F., Hicham M., Adil S. (2016). Information security risk assessment—A practical approach with a mathematical formulation of risk. International Journal of Computer Applications, 103(8), 89–99.

Mohamed N., Nawawi A., Ismail I. S., Ahmad S. A., Azmi N. A., Zakaria N. B. (2013). Cyber fraud challenges and the analysts competency: Evidence from digital forensic department of cyber security Malaysia. Recent Trends in Social Sciences-Proceedings of the 2nd International Congress on Interdisciplinary Behavior and Social Sciences, 3(2), 581–583.

Molok N. N. A., Ahmad A., Chang S. (2018). A case analysis of securing organisations against information leakage through online social networking. International Journal of Information Management, 43(4), 351–356.

Muhammad S., Maimoona S., Alain F., Norizan J. (2018). Impact of service quality on customer satisfaction in Malaysia airlines: A PLS-SEM approach. Journal of Air Transport Management, 67(1), 169–180.

Mustaruddin S., Norhayah Z., Rusnah M. (2010). Malaysian corporate social responsibility disclosure and its relation on institutional ownership. Managerial Auditing Journal, 2(6), 349–350.

Myyry L., Siponen M., Pahnila S., Vartiainen A. (2009). What levels of moral reasoning and values explain adherence to information security rules? An empirical study. European Journal of Information Systems, 18(2), 126–139.

Nader S., Safa R., Solms L. (2016). Human aspects of information security in organizations. Computer Fraud & Security, 3(2), 15–18.

Ned K. (2016). Common method bias in PLS-SEM: A full collinearity assessment approach. International Journal of e-Collaboration, 5(2), 70–89.

Neeta S., Sachin K. (2014). A comparative study on information security risk analysis practices. International Journal of Computer Applications, 11(3), 123–139.

Nik Z., Azlinah M., Noor H. (2010). Information security risk factors: Critical threats vulnerabilities in ICT outsourcing. IEEE, 23(4), 65–79.

Nik Z., Azlinah M., Noor H. (2013). ICT outsourcing information security risk factors: An exploratory analysis of threat risks factor for critical project characteristics. Journal of Industrial and Intelligent Information, 1(4), 44–59.

Nik Z., Noor H., Azlinah M. (2010). Conceptual framework on information security risk management in information technology. Journal of Media and Information Warfare, 3(4), 77–104.

Nik Z., Shekh A. (2018). Legal protection of Intellectual Property Rights (IPR) in Bangladesh. International Journal of Law. Government and Communication, 3(12), 71–89.

Nik Z., Shekh A. (2019). Toward fact- based digital forensic evidence collection methodology. International Journal for Information Security Research (IJISR), 9(1), 67–79.

Nik Z., Shekh A., Tan T. (2018). Viewpoint of probabilistic risk assessment in artificial enabled social engineering attacks. BITARA International Journal of Civilizational Studies and Human Sciences, 1(4), 32–39.

Nikolaos A., Konstantinos A., Haralambos M., Andrew F. (2017). Decision-making in security requirements engineering with constrained goal models. Computer Security, 34(2), 262–280.

Noor H., Azlinah M. (2010a). Information technology governance practices in Malaysian public sector. IEEE, 2(1), 44–56.

Noor H., Azlinah M. (2010b). IT governance practices model in IT project approval and implementation in Malaysian public sector. IEEE, 12(1), 442–456.

Noor H., Azlinah M. (2012). Chaos issues on communication in agile global software development. IEEE Business, 6(2), 55–68.

Noor H., Yap M., Azlinah M. (2007) Inherent risks in ICT. Proceeding of the 8th WSEAS Conference, 8(1), 141–146.

Otway H., von Wintcrfeldt D. (1999). Expert judgment in risk analysis and management: Process, context, and pitfalls. The Journal of Risk Analysis, 12(1), 83–93.

Papadaki K., Nineta P. (2015). Towards a systematic approach for improving information security risk management methods. IEEE 18th International Symposium on Personal, Indoor and Mobile Radio Communications, 4(2), 55–61.

Parker Donn B. (2014). Toward a new framework for information security, computer security handbook. New York, NY: John Wiley & Sons.

Patton M. Q. (2004). Two decades of developments in qualitative inquiry: A personal, experiential perspective. Journal of Developmental Child Welfare, 1(3), 261–283.

Peltier T. R. (2006). Social engineering: Concepts and solutions. Information Systems Security, 15(5), 13–21.

Peltier T. R. (2012). Information security risk analysis. 3rd ed., CRC Press, Taylor & Francis Group.

Peltier T. R. (2016). Information security policies, procedures, and standards: Guidelines for effective information security management. Taylor & Francis Group.

Poppo L., Zenger T. (1998). Testing alternative theories of the finn: Transaction cost, knowledge- based, and measurement explanations in information services. Strategic Management Journal, 19(9), 853–862.

Posey C., Roberts T., Lowry P. (2015). The impact of organizational commitment on insiders' motivation to protect organizational information assets. Journal of Management Information Systems, 32(4), 179–214.

Price Waterhouse Coopers. (2010). Information security breach survey. Journal of Current Research in Computing, 4(2), 67–73.

Radhakrisna G. (2014). Digital evidence in Malaysia. Journal of Digital Evidence and Electronic Signature Law Review, 31(5), 220–240.

Ramirez R., Choucri N. (2016). Improving interdisciplinary communication with standardized cyber security terminology: A literature review. IEEE Access, 4, 2216–2243.

Rossouw V., Solms J., Niekerk. (2014). From information security to cyber security. Computers & Security, 38(4), 97–102.

Sameer H., Bharanidharan S., Ganthan N., Norbik B., Azuan A. (2014). Security risk assessment framework for cloud computing environments. Wiley Online Library, 7(11), 114–124.

Sandelowski M. (2013). Focus on research method, combining qualitative and quantitative sampling, data collection, and analysis techniques in mixed-method studies. Research in Nursing and Health, 23(1), 246–255.

Selcaran U. (2016). Research methods for business. 5th ed., New York, NY: John Wiley and Sons.

Shaukat K., Luo S., Varadharajan V., Hameed I. A., Xu M. (2020). A survey on machine learning techniques for cyber security in the last decade. IEEE Access, 8, 222310–222354.

Shaun P., Rossouw V. (2006). A framework for the governance of information security. Computers & Security, 23(8), 638–646.

Shekh A. (2018). Mobile device security. 1E- Proceeding of the 1st International MedLit Media Literacy for Social Change Conference 2018, 2(1), 342–350.

Shekh A. (2019). Security of electronic mail system, Folio, FTKW Magazine.

Shekh A., Nik Z. (2018). An exploratory factor analysis of AI enabled Social Engineering (SoE) attacking risk in higher learning institute. Journal of Mass Communication & Journalism, 15(1), 32–40.

Shekh A., Nik Z., Tan T. (2018). An investigation of AI enabled Social Engineering (SoE) attacking impact in higher learning institute: Structural Equation Modeling (SEM)Approach. Journal of Applied & Computational Mathematics, 23(2), 562–570.

Shekh A., Nik Z., Tan T. (2019a). Towards the big data and digital evidence integrity. Journal of Intelek, 14(1), 56–63.

Shekh A., Nik Z., Tan T. (2019b). Toward the data security and digital evidence-based solution in Bangladesh perspective. ZULFAQAR International Journal of Defense Science, Engineering & Technology, 21(1), 19–20.

Singh R. (2015). Kali Linux social engineering—effectively perform efficient and organized social engineering tests and penetration testing using Kali Linux. Packt Publishing Inc. Ltd.

Singleton T. W., Singleton A. J. (2014). The potential for a synergistic relationship between information security and a financial audit. Information Security Journal: A Global Perspective, 17(2), 80–86.

Siti Rahayu S., Robiah Y., Shahrin S. (2014). Malaysian mapping process of digital forensic investigation framework. International Journal of Computer Science and Network Security, 8(10), 26–35.

Suci R., Yasmirah M., Robbi R., Andysah P. (2017). Post-genesis digital forensics investigation. International Journal of Science and Technology, 3(6), 123–133.

Suit H. (2008). Information System (IS) analysis based on a business model. Journal of Global Information Management, 14(3), 39–49.

Sumner M. (2011). Information security threats: A comparative analysis of impact, probability, and preparedness. Information Systems Management, 26(1), 2–12.

Sun X., Yu F. R., Zhang P. (2022). A survey on cyber-security of Connected and Autonomous Vehicles (CAVs). IEEE Transactions on Intelligent Transportation Systems, 23(7), 6240–6259.

Sundresan Perumal. (2009). Digital forensic model based on Malaysian investigation process. International Journal of Computer Science and Network Security, 9(8), 119–126.

Taylor P. J., Dargahi T., Dehghantanha A. (2021). A systematic literature review of blockchain cyber security. Digital Communications and Networks, 6(2), 147–156.

Teixeira A., Amin S., Sandberg H., Johansson K. H., Sastry S. S. (2010). Cyber security analysis of state estimators in electric power systems. 49th IEEE Conference on Decision and Control (CDC), Atlanta, GA, 5991–5998.

Ten C.-W., Liu C.-C., Manimaran G. (2008). Vulnerability assessment of cybersecurity for SCADA systems. IEEE Transactions on Power Systems, 23(4), 1836–1846.

Ten C.-W., Manimaran G., Liu C.-C. (2010). Cybersecurity for critical infrastructures: Attack and defense modeling. IEEE Transactions on Systems, Man, and Cybernetics—Part A: Systems and Humans, 40(4), 853–865.

Thakur K., Qiu M., Gai K., Ali M. L. (2015). An investigation on cyber security threats and security models. IEEE 2nd International Conference on Cyber Security and Cloud Computing, 307–311.

Todd F. (2016). Physical security. Handbook of Information Security Management. Taylor & Francis Group.

Ullah F., Naeem H., Jabbar S., Khalid S., Latif M. A. (2017). Cyber security threats detection in internet of things using deep learning approach. IEEE Access, 7, 124379–124389.

Veiga A., Eloff J. (2009). An information security governance framework. Information Systems Management, 24(4), 361–372.

Vorster A., Labuschagne L. (2009). A framework for comparing different information security risk analysis methodologies. ACM Digital Library, 28(4), 651–667.

Wiafe I., Koranteng F. N., Obeng E. N., Assyne N., Wiafe A., Gulliver S. R. (2020). Artificial intelligence for cybersecurity: A systematic mapping of literature. IEEE Access, 8, 146598–146612.

Wiebke A. (2009). Agents, trojans and tags: The next generation of investigators. International Review of Law, Computers & Technology, 23(1–2), 99–108.

Xin Y., Kong L., Liu Z., Chen Y., Li Y., Zhu H., Gao M. (2018). Machine learning and deep learning methods for cybersecurity. IEEE Access, 6, 35365–35381.

Yamin M. M., Katt B. (2022). Modeling and executing cyber security exercise scenarios in cyber ranges. Computers & Security, 116, 56–70.

Yang Y., Littler T., Sezer S., McLaughlin K., Wang H. F. (2011). Impact of cybersecurity issues on smart grid. *IEEE PES International Conference and Exhibition on Innovative Smart Grid Technologies*, Manchester, UK, 1–7

Zhang J., Pan L., Han Q.-L., Chen C., Wen S., Xiang Y. (2022). Deep learning based attack detection for cyber-physical system cybersecurity: A Survey. IEEE/CAA Journal of Automatica Sinica, 9(3), 377–391.

Zwilling M., Klien G., Lesjak D., Wiechetek Ł. (2022). Cyber security awareness, knowledge and behavior: A comparative study. Journal of Computer Information Systems, 62(1), 82–97.

Index

VR, *see* virtual reality (VR)
VRM, *see* Vendor Risk Management
        (VRM)
vulnerability identification, 107

W

WhatsApp, 63
white hat hacker, 157
worm, 52–53

Y

Yahoo, 57

Z

ZeroGPT AI Content Detector, 86
zero-knowledge proofs (ZKPs), 141, 159
Zero Trust Architecture, 55
ZKPs, *see* zero-knowledge proofs (ZKPs)

Printed in the United States
by Baker & Taylor Publisher Services